ENGLISH ANTIQUES

Royal Worcester horn-shaped 'Ryton' vase, 1878
Royal Worcester Porcelain Co. Ltd.

English Antiques

Compiled and edited by

G. E. Speck and Euan Sutherland

WARD LOCK LIMITED · LONDON

Made and printed in Great Britain by
William Clowes and Sons, Limited, London and Beccles

EDITORS' NOTE

English Antiques cover the most popular aspects of collecting as far as the beginner is concerned—and this work is essentially for the newcomer to the world of antiques. Preparing such a work presents a host of problems not the least being to produce a book whose price is not beyond the pocket of those for whom the work is specifically intended. To get over this all-too-real problem the editors have drawn on the well-known 'Creative Leisure Books' and 'Collectors Monographs', both of which they were closely involved in initiating and editing. Incidentally, the editors are fully responsible for all facts and opinions.

Each subject is prefaced by an essay that covers the essentials of the subject—certainly sufficient not only to whet the appetite of the beginner but to inform him whether or not the subject is truly of interest and to his taste. For the reader who wishes to pursue the subject there is a reasonably comprehensive book list at the end of this work. However, what will be of great interest and value are the many choice specimens reproduced in the work. To the beginner—and the experienced collector—the important thing is visual identity, knowing what a specific style looks like so that it can be accurately identified at a later date. Further, the examples selected are not exclusively museum specimens, many are of excellent quality and style and, what is important, available from dealers and auction galleries. There is nothing more frustrating than looking at page after page of photographs not one example of which is available either because they are in a museum or are so rare that only a Greek shipping millionaire or Texan oilman can ever consider owning them.

Firstly, we would like to acknowledge our debt to the many museums, private collectors and dealers who so generously supplied the photographs reproduced in this work; in many cases the acknowledgement is given at the end of the caption. Secondly, and most significantly, we would like to express our extreme indebtedness to Stanley W. Fisher (ceramics), Judith Banister (silver), Sydney Crompton (glass), Frederick Wilkinson (small arms, swords and daggers) and E. J. Tyler (clocks). Without their writings and expertise this book would not have been possible.

Victorian oil lamp.

CONTENTS

A London or Bristol Delft charger with a portrait of James II in blue, purple and yellow. It dates from about 1680.
Victoria & Albert Museum

A Delft posset-pot. It was made at Lambeth about 1700. The decoration is a crude interpretation of Chinese motifs and is in blue, red and green.

CERAMICS

There is no record of the beginnings of the craft of making vessels of clay for use as food or drink containers—of the early progression through the stages of baking in the sun, firing in a kiln, shaping by hand, throwing on a primitive potter's wheel, glazing to secure imperviousness to liquids, and decorating at the potter's untutored whim. It is clear, however, that at some time or other, at different periods in different countries, the early kiln-baked clays which we call earthenwares were improved upon in different ways. Thus, an earthenware made of some kind of natural clay was subjected to a much higher kiln temperature to become stoneware—a much harder vitrified material which was impervious to water—while the addition of other substances, notably china-clay (kaolin) and china-stone (petuntse) was found to give the translucency which is the distinguishing feature of porcelain. Certain non-porosity and added beauty was given by a protecting layer of glaze (or glass), which was probably an early Egyptian invention, and which is found with few exceptions upon all three bodies—earthenware, stoneware and porcelain.

In England the Romans made much fine pottery, but on their departure the craft was continued only by itinerant potters, of whom there are no records, who worked wherever they found suitable clay until local needs had been supplied. This medieval pottery was usually clumsy, often misshapen, and covered with a lead glaze in green, brown or yellow. Decoration was mainly incised (or scratched), impressed or applied in the form of shaped pads of clay. Apparently the potter used for this purpose anything that came to hand, bits of twig, sea-shells, nails and so on, but some innate sense of craftsmanship and design always prevented him from obscuring the plastic nature of the clay. There were of course no decorators, as we understand the term, in those days.

It was during the fifteenth century that potteries were established at many centres, among them London, Wrotham in Kent, in Staffordshire, Derbyshire and Cheshire. Decoration in colour was introduced, notably in the form of applied decoration in contrasting colours which led up to the popularity of what are known as *slip wares* in the seventeenth century. This kind of pottery, which is associated particularly with a family of Staffordshire potters by the name of Toft, is today rare and valuable. It has no delicacy and was never intended to be other than utilitarian. The simple process of manufacture was that upon a red clay body a mixture of white clay and water (*slip* as it is called) was worked into patterns of wavy and dotted lines, flowers and leaves, animals and birds, and crude human figures and busts, before the whole was covered with lead glaze. Many important pieces bear names which may be either those of the makers or of intended recipients.

Towards the end of the seventeenth century, as some faint glimmerings of Far-Eastern culture began to spread to Europe, a handful of potters began to experiment with stoneware, in imitation of the ware then being made by a Meissen (Dresden) potter named Johann Böttger, who in turn had already copied from the Chinese. The best known of them are John Dwight of Fulham, who perfected a lovely white stoneware, and John and David Elers, whose red or black ware was lathe-turned in formal geometrical patterns, or else bore applied ornament which had been stamped out in metal dies. This *sprigged* decoration was developed to a high degree by John Astbury, an early eighteenth-century potter who worked very much in the Elers style, though his ware was glazed whereas Astbury's was not.

Though no glaze was really needed on stoneware, another class of seventeenth-century ware is known by the name of *salt-glazed*, because it was glazed with salt thrown into the kiln at a temperature of over two thousand degrees Fahrenheit; this resulted in the characteristic, slightly pitted, orange-skin appearance. The white surface of the early ware was sometimes enhanced by the addition of incised design which was then filled in with blue pigment. Stoneware was further developed right into the eighteenth century, culminating in a spate of colourful, jewel-like enamelling in the Chinese and continental styles, but at the same time lead-glazed pottery was improved to a high degree. Whieldon made figures and also perfected the use of mingled glazes in different colours in what are known as his 'tortoiseshell' wares. While with Wedgwood he used a fine green glaze on moulded articles such as the well-known 'cauliflower' tea-pots and tea-caddies, on which it contrasted to perfection with the creamy-white body. During the eighteenth century, too, Ralph Wood of Burslem followed the Astbury tradition in the making of mantelpiece figures and the familiar Toby jug—to be followed by his descendants and many others who developed the Staffordshire Figures which are so popular today.

Early in the eighteenth century attempts were made at imitating Chinese porcelain; this resulted in the making of what is known as 'delft' in Holland and in our own country, 'majolica' in Italy and Spain and 'faience' in Germany and France. The only similarity between porcelain and delft lay in the white surface colour of each and in the kind of decoration, in Chinese style, which was applied to it, for whereas porcelain is translucent, delft is not, being merely ordinary earthenware covered with a white tin-oxide based glaze, the powdery texture of which demanded bold, clean brushwork. We speak of the 'delft painter's touch' when we consider this kind of necessarily coarse decoration, which is to be found upon the delft made between about 1600 and 1770 at London, Bristol and Liverpool.

So far as translucent porcelain proper is concerned, it is known that certain continental potters experimented successfully as early as 1580, but not until 1710 was

A slipware jug with date around the neck. It has a light-brown body with the design picked out with white dots. The bird and flowers were laid down in areas of reddish-brown clay and the whole covered with a colourless lead glaze.

The Bell Works, Burslem.

anything done on a large scale; it was at Meissen that Böttger found out that the true porcelain of the Far East was composed of a mixture of china-clay and china-stone. Then, in 1745, the chemists at Vincennes evolved their own kind of porcelain, an imitation made of china-clay and a *fritt* of powdered glass which we now call *soft paste* or 'artificial' porcelain. It was this kind of substitute which our own potters, working independently and without any kind of Royal or State patronage, one by one invented. At Bow, Thomas Frye and Edward Heylyn took out a patent in 1744 and a factory was established at Chelsea perhaps even a little earlier. These were followed soon after 1750 by rival concerns at Bristol, Worcester, Derby, Lowestoft, Liverpool and Longton Hall in Staffordshire—all making soft-paste porcelains of different compositions. Then, in 1768, William Cookworthy found out how to make true porcelain, probably quite by accident, and set up a factory in Plymouth which was later moved to Bristol and finally, so far as its secrets and methods were concerned, to New Hall in the Potteries.

Every now and then innovators tried with varying degrees of success to market new *pastes* (bodies) which were better than the others. Thus, in the 1820s, William Billingsley, chemist and china-painter, invented a wonderfully beautiful paste which he made at Pinxton, Nantgarw and Swansea until at length ruinous kiln losses brought failure and a return to the old position of paid decorator in another's factory. The same kind of attempts were made elsewhere, resulting often in unrivalled beauty and technical perfection but in bankruptcy also. The established factories introduced paste after paste, always striving after perfection, until with all the resources of the great potting centre of Staffordshire behind them, Spodes perfected and introduced, soon after 1800, a new body in which china-clay and china-stone were reinforced with calcined bone or *bone-ash*. It was not long before variations of this new paste had replaced every other kind, and there has been little change in its composition since.

When our potters first made porcelain they had no previous experience in the decorating

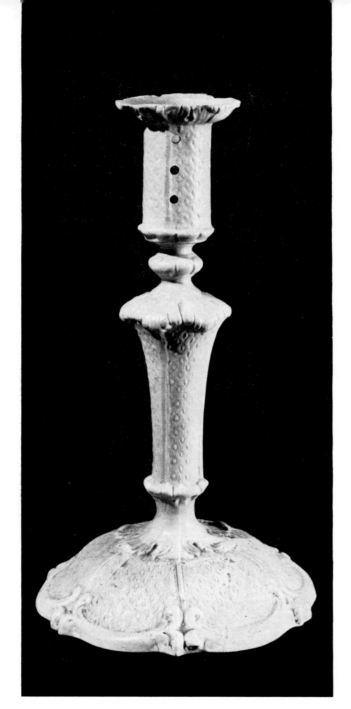

A Staffordshire salt-glazed candlestick, made about 1730. Its style derives from an original in silver. The piece was moulded in two parts as evidenced by the visible join down its length.

A pear-shaped Liverpool Delft vase with a tipped rim. The decoration of flowers and rock is in the Fazackerly style.

Sotheby & Co.

of it, for the old styles which suited earthenware were quite unsuited to the much more delicate ware. It is true that now and again, on Liverpool wares in particular, we recognise the bold brushwork of a delft painter, but by and large the decoration on early English porcelain was the result of a new technique, and the popular styles were copied from alien sources. At first, because Chinese porcelain was so popular and familiar, at least among the educated and well-to-do, decoration was carried out in the Chinese style, in blue or in enamels. Occasionally the exotic Oriental designs were exactly copied, but more usually the separate motifs, the mandarin figures, the flowering shrubs, the dragons, the pagodas and so on were used in endless combinations to form the kind of patterns which Europeans expected to see. The much hackneyed *Willow Pattern*, though of later date, is a typical example of the kind of decoration which no Chinese artist could possibly ever perpetrate. Very few Japanese patterns were copied, apart from those in the style of a seventeenth-century potter named Kakiemon, which may be seen on Worcester and Bow porcelains in particular, under such nicknames as 'wheatsheaf', 'banded hedge', 'quail' and 'partridge'.

From the famous Meissen factory, on the outskirts of Dresden, much fine porcelain was exported to England, and its designs (many of which were adaptations of Chinese originals) were copied by our decorators between about 1760 and 1770 while at the same time the Oriental taste fell gradually into disfavour. The German styles which quickly became popular included European landscapes and harbour scenes and naturalistic birds; but above all the greatest influence on British porcelain decoration was in the forms of flowers and the wonderfully colourful, entirely imaginary creatures known as 'exotic birds', which at Worcester, rendered in different styles by innumerable artists, were reserved upon scale-blue grounds to splendidly brilliant effect. The flower painting took three distinct forms, formal Oriental flowers (*Indianische Blumen*),

A Royal Worcester 'first period' vase. The paintings are on a scale-blue ground. Its date is about 1770.

Royal Worcester Porcelain Co. Ltd.

naturalistic flowers (*Streu Blumen*), and bouquets and sprigs of idealised flowers (*Meissner Blumen*). During the time of this predominance of the German styles it was inevitable that the influence of the second great continental factory at Sèvres should occasionally have some effect on English design, and when the Meissen concern was taken over by the Prussians in 1763 the resultant disorganisation gave the French their chance to oust their rivals as dictators of fashion in porcelain decoration. The effect, between 1770 and the end of the century, is seen on our wares in the shape of a spate of wonderful ground (all-over) colours such as *bleu-de-roi, bleu celeste* (turquoise), apple, pea and sea-greens, and *Rose Pompadour* (claret), allied often to magnificent gilded patterning of every kind. We see too, on Chelsea, Derby and Worcester wares in particular, a great variety of daintily gay arrangements of floral and foliate festoons, seen to typical effect in the Worcester 'hop trellis' patterns.

Porcelain decoration after 1800, when there was marked acceleration of the change from individuality to commercialism, is too vast and complex a subject to be adequately described in these pages. With technical difficulties more or less overcome there was no limit to possible extravagance in decoration, and extravagance was in fact often welcomed by a new kind of public who could afford the best and who wanted its value to be obvious. The porcelain body was used more and more merely as a canvas to receive fine painting in every conceivable style, and though sometimes the older, still-flourishing factories such as Derby and Worcester carried on their old traditions of restrained design, even in their wares technical perfection may sometimes seem a poor exchange for the inexplicable but real attraction of their imperfect early productions—at least in the eyes of the collector. At the beginning, of course, few factories had their own staff of proficient, trained decorators, and special or difficult work was often entrusted to 'outside decorators' in London or elsewhere, whereas every nineteenth-century factory of any importance had its own properly trained artists, many of them specialists, and many of them known to us by their styles and, sometimes, by their names. The result is that the collector of later wares must perforce be interested more in decoration than in the paste upon which it rests, particularly since this was more or less standardised throughout the industry.

A salt-glaze teapot, c. 1750. The decoration is mainly blue and painted directly upon a bright red ground.

A Staffordshire salt-glaze 'owl' jug and stand; the head is a detachable cup. The modelling of the form recalls Picasso in his most primitive style.

Sotheby & Co.

Above, *the State Drawing-room of Osborne House, Queen Victoria's favourite house.* Left, *a typical mid-Victorian music cover. Note the sentimental pose and fascination with the exotic.*

Left, *a mid-seventeenth century dish-hilt rapier.* Right, *an officer's small sword complete with sword knot. Dated c. 1800.*

A powder tester by John Manton and one of a pair of brass-framed tap-action pistols by Jackson of Market Harborough. Both from the Rabbet Collection.

Three salt-glaze stoneware jugs.
Left: *white, blue and dark brown on a light slip ground; by George Tinworth 1874.*
Centre: *light and dark blues and white on a buff slip ground; by Arthur B. Barlow.*
Right: *light and dark blues, white and dark brown on a pale-green slip ground; by George Tinworth, c. 1874*

A Wedgwood creamware jug with black-printed decoration typical of these jugs which were made in many factories in the Potteries during the early part of the nineteenth century.
Wedgwood & Sons Ltd.

A Leeds creamware chest-
nut bowl, cover and stand.
Note the delicate piercing
which was a characteristic
of the Leeds factory. Made
around 1800.
Victoria & Albert Museum.

Staffordshire cream-
ware plate and one of a
set of the 'Seven Ages
of Man'. It was prob-
ably decorated by a
Dutchman working in
the Potteries. It is dated
about 1770.

DEN DOOP

Staffordshire white creamware chestnut bowl, cover and stand.
Note the delicate flower heads at the terminals of the twisted
rope handles. This piece is marked 'John Daniel' 1775.

British Museum.

Wedgwood
'nautilus' centre
piece and stand.
It was decorated
from Wedg-
wood's pattern
book of 1770
and is marked
'Wedgwood'.
The service of
which this is a
part was made
at Etruria in
1798.

Wedgwood & Sons
Ltd.

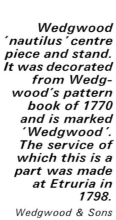

A Staffordshire creamware plate of Lord Nelson. During the first half of the nineteenth century there was a ready sale for pieces bearing the portraits of notabilities.
British Museum.

Left: Wedgwood blue jasper centrepiece with yellow and white strapwork. It dates from 1790. Right: Wedgwood white jasper dish with blue, yellow and white strapwork, 1740.
Wedgwood & Sons Ltd.

Wedgwood early morning tea-set. The decoration is a white relief on a blue jasper ground. The pieces date from 1784.
Wedgwood & Sons Ltd.

*Late nineteenth century
Copeland (Late Spode)
dish. The blue-painting
was by Charles F. Hürten.*

W. T. Copeland and Sons Ltd.

*Three pieces of Mason's ironstone china.
Decorated in the Chinese style; c. 1830–40.*

*An Astbury-Whieldon figure of a seated piper. These rather
simply modelled figures were popular about 1745.*

A Ralph Wood Toby
jug of the 'Thin
Man'. These were
copied well into the
nineteenth century.

An extremely rare pair of Bow monkeys.
They date from the period 1757–58.

Antique Porcelain Co. Ltd.

A delightful pair of Chelsea bocage candlestick figures
of the red-anchor period, about 1755. The bases are
modelled in the popular 'rococo' style.

A Chelsea tureen of the red anchor period 1755–60.
Fitzwilliam Museum.

A Worcester sauce-boat dating from about 1760- 65.
Royal Worcester Porcelain Co. Ltd.

A Worcester tureen, cover and stand decorated in underglaze blue and enamels in a design based on Japanese Imari ware. It can be dated about 1770.

A hexagonal Worcester vase and cover with underglaze blue-painted decoration in Meissen/Chinese style. It is marked with the crossed swords of Meissen and dates around 1765–70.

Derby heart-shaped dish with underglaze-blue decoration in the Chinese style. It was made about 1760.

A Blood Derby jug of the Bloor period and probably made between 1825 and 1880. Pieces like this are often credited to Coleport or Rockingham.

A Lowestoft bowl made about 1765. The landscape design is blue and the borders are typical of Lowestoft 'white and blue'.

A Lowestoft coffee-pot, c. 1757–60. It is decorated in underglaze blue in a typical Chinese style.

Sotheby & Co.

A Longton Hall sauce-boat of the middle period, c. 1754–57.
Antique Porcelain Company Ltd.

A Longton Hall leaf dish which can be dated c. 1755–60.

A pair of Longton Hall figures representing 'Harlequin' and 'Columbine'. They date from about 1755.

A Liverpool cup and saucer made by Chaffers. The Chinese design is in underglaze blue. Date c. 1758–60.

A Liverpool bowl. The exterior is painted with a landscape but the interior of the bowl is of the frigate 'Hyena'. It may be dated c. 1775–80.

Christie, Manson & Woods Ltd.

Set of Caughley tea-wares. They are underglaze blue printed and date from around 1775.

This Coalport teapot and cover was made about 1830 although it carries the mark 'Swansea'.

*A medieval mazer of the fifteenth century;
the foot is later and is dated about 1620.*
British Museum.

*The Hutton Cup, a communion
cup, made in 1589. Tradition
has it that the cup was given
to Elizabeth Bowes by Queen
Elizabeth I for her wedding.
The restrained decoration
is from Renaissance designs.*
Christie, Manson & Woods Ltd.

SILVER

Since medieval times English silversmiths have eagerly assimilated the styles and manners of Continental designers and craftsmen. Yet English silver is almost always unmistakably English.

By far the greatest quantity of English silver was made in London, although there are long and strong traditions of craftsmanship in other parts of the country. Exeter, Chester, Newcastle, York and many other towns were centres of silversmithing for many centuries. Now, of the provincial assay offices where silver has to be tested and marked, only Birmingham and Sheffield, both set up in 1773, are left outside London.

London, as the centre of commerce and culture, always attracted wealth, and where there is wealth there are goldsmiths and silversmiths. During the seventeenth century wealthy goldsmiths often concerned themselves with usury and with banking, and even during the eighteenth century not a few silversmiths advertised that they kept 'running cashes'. This was, in fact, quite a logical situation. Gold and silver were, in effect, so much bullion that happened to be on hand in a pleasant and useful form.

The patron of the silversmith still tended to look on his plate as a sort of public bank-balance. After all, it was of the same sterling standard as the coinage, so conversion was simple enough. In the same way, if he grew tired of the design of his silver (often known as *white plate*) or his silver-gilt (carelessly dubbed *gold* or *gilt*), then he just had it remade in the current fashion.

The Restoration of Charles II in 1660 is usually considered the beginning of the era of domestic silver. The Church during the Middle Ages had been the patron of the arts, but the ravages of the Reformation had taken a heavy toll of medieval treasures. Added to that there had been the heavy demands of war over the centuries, the lavish gifts made to foreign potentates and, finally, the wholesale destruction of plate to support one side or the other during the Civil War—quite apart from wear and tear and the common habit of melting plate to have it refashioned. For the collector pre-Restoration silver, even small articles such as spoons, beakers, tumbler cups and wine tasters, are often beyond reach. This is not to suggest that silver of the medieval, Tudor and early Stuart periods should be ignored.

The Renaissance, which came late to England and did not make much impact on silver until the 1530s, was the source of all European design tradition for centuries to come. Its decoration, based on revived classicism, with flutes and acanthus leafage, swags of fruit, flowers and scrolls, satisfied the appetite of artists virtually until the mid-eighteenth century when its themes became out of hand, and it needed Adam and the neo-classicists to formalise its motifs by returning to the ancient originals once more.

The influences on English silver, from Holbein at the court of Henry VIII to that of Van Vianen at Charles I's court, were always European. Foreign silversmiths working in London and elsewhere were no phenomenon.

There was during and immediately after the Civil War a break in the history of the craft. For more than a decade before the return of Charles II the trade, in London at any rate, was virtually in abeyance.

The Restoration coincided with new developments in science and industry, art and architecture, trade and overseas enterprise. Those who had joined the royal family in exile returned and set about rebuilding their houses, farming the new estates assigned to loyal supporters, and replenishing their stores of plate. There were the large and prosperous middle classes, all quite prepared to emulate their wealthier neighbours. For the silversmith, the return of Charles II in May, 1660, was the beginning of a long era of work and prosperity. With trade at its lowest ebb there were problems, but the craft promptly celebrated the occasion by deciding to change the annual date-letter (struck on all plate) from the traditional May 19th, St. Dunstan's Day, to May 29th, the King's birthday.

With the Restoration came an upsurge of demand for bold and showy silver and silver-gilt. As usual, the impetus came from abroad, and now, the returning court brought new styles home with them. Both France and Holland wielded great influence on silver design. Louis XIV was still a young man, but his famous 'L'état, c'est moi' was a dictum already five years old. In Holland, there was the impact of the floral baroque. The swirled and lobed style of Van Vianen gave way to exuberant flowers and foliage, birds and animals—still bold, still with the emphasis on embossing and chasing, but reflecting the Dutch interest in natural history.

The two-handled cups, variously called porringers, caudle cups and posset cups, are probably the most typical of all Charles II silverwares. Posset and caudle were both spiced milk drinks, curdled with wine or ale and taken hot, so that handled cups were very necessary. The rather squat bulging bodies of these cups were usually embossed and chased with flowers, foliage and animals. A lion on one side and a unicorn on the other —sometimes varied by bears, hounds, deer,

A 'snuffer' tray made by Francis Garthorne, a London goldsmith, in 1678.

boars, goats and the like coursing round the sides amid the foliage—were popular motifs, the bold style of the embossing serving to conceal the rather thin metal. Silver remained in short supply, and demand was heavy, and did not wane. A typical feature of the bulging-bodied porringers was the cast caryatid handles, which became progressively more spindly and more formalised, so that some appear as slender, double scrolls with leafy blobs for heads instead of curvaceous maidens.

Standing cups were made again, sometimes in styles that harked back to the originals that had been melted down. Occasionally, replicas of the great standing salts were made—mostly in the capstan shape on a circular or square base with a waisted spool support for the salt, and with scrolls which presumably held a napkin to keep the salt covered. But the days of the high table were virtually over, so that silver for show was more likely to be in the form of garnitures for the mantelpiece or fireplace—vases and jars with no other purpose but to gleam and look splendid in firelight and candlelight. Between ten and fifteen inches high, they are typically enriched with floral and foliate embossing enclosing cherubs or masks and

Left *and* right, two Bristol Blue decanters with pear-shaped stoppers and gilded labels. Centre, *a green spirit decanter. In the foreground two Bristol Blue wineglasses.*

Left, *a late silver rococo tea-caddy, made by Nicholas Hearnden, 1769. Centre, an oval teapot of fluted drum form, 1788. Right, a coffee-pot by Peter Archambo, 1738. The scissor-tongs were made by John Frost about 1760.*

Above, *an English pewter dish, c. 1640, a William & Mary (left) domed-lid tankard, c. 1690, a capstan-shaped salt (centre), c. 1695 and a Charles II flagon (right), c. 1730. Below, a First Period Worcester tureen in the form of billing doves, about 1760.*

with richly festooned applied work round the necks.

Equally richly ornamented were the silver sconces for one or two candles, with shaped oval back-plates, and the impressive toilet services with perhaps a dozen or sixteen pieces, including mirror, jewel caskets, pin cushion, flasks, flagons and dishes and even covered bowls elaborately chased with scrolls, leafage and *amorini* in high relief.

Not all Charles II silver was rich and gaudy. There had been a leavening in the French style of cut-card work introduced about 1650. Cut-card ornament, consisting of thin silhouettes of silver soldered round the bases of bowls and cups, and round finials and handle sockets, was an effective way of helping to strengthen thin-gauge metal. Some silver, notably tankards, wine cups and the heavy-based small tumbler cups, on the whole escaped the current passion for overall decoration, other than perhaps a band of acanthus leaf chasing or an engraved coat-of-arms in a plumed mantling.

In the Commonwealth period, the beer tankard had a spreading base, aptly called a skirt foot, and replaced the so-called 'Puritan' type with its base in one with the body and without a foot. By 1660, the rim foot and a slightly tapering cylindrical barrel established the type of tankard that was to be little changed for more than half a century. Unlike the handles on bowls and cups, tankard handles were broad scrolls, sometimes with hoof-like terminals, and with a cast, bifurcated or two-lobed thumbpiece.

Baroque style heavy cap and cover. On the basis of its style it can be dated about 1680.
G. S. Sanders, Esq.

Tankards were almost always covered, the lid being a flat-domed cap with a small wavy or pointed peak at the front. Base and lip were usually simply moulded or reeded. Incidentally, the small holes found at the base of the scroll handles, sometimes shaped rather like the mouthpiece of a wind instrument, were simply blow-holes to allow the air to escape when the handle was soldered on.

Wine cups, soon to be ousted by glasses, were also of the styles most copied in glass. They had a trumpet-shaped bowl and simple baluster stem on a circular moulded foot. Following a really old-established tradition were the small beakers, made in various

Oval casket with cut-card decoration above the cast feet and round the looped snake handle.
Irwin Untermeyer

Left: *a beaker of the type widely used until the coming of glass at the end of the seventeenth century. It is engraved by a maker with the mark 'GC' for the Mitchell family of Hamp, Somerset.*
Below: *two flagons made in 1646 which are outstanding examples of mid-seventeenth century chasing in the Dutch style.*
Below left: *tankard in the Elizabeth Renaissance style. It carries the mark 'RP' and London hallmark for 1638.*
Victoria & Albert Museum.

sizes from about two and a half to seven inches high. They had cylindrical bodies flaring to the rims, and might be plain or decorative as taste and money dictated. Another commonplace in silver were the delightful little tumbler cups which were probably used for spirits or other strong liquors. Rarely more than a couple of inches high, they are heavy-based so that they return to upright even if tilted.

About 1670 several new styles made their appearance in England, though of them only acanthus leafage and fluted baroque (also of Dutch derivation) survived to the end of the century, given new impetus with the arrival of Dutch William on the throne of England.

The baroque was really a formalising of the Dutch naturalistic style. The emphasis was still on embossing and chasing, but they became more restrained. Alternating palm and acanthus leaf chasing was arranged around the bases of cups and tankards, or round the broad rims of dishes. Fluting, both straight and swirled, was similarly used on the lower parts of drinking vessels, and it was a style admirably suited to the column candlesticks of the period, which gradually became plainer until ousted by the cast baluster candlestick in the 1680s.

One unusual and rather rare style used for display plate was to make a tankard or cup quite plain, gild it and then sheathe it with a pierced and chased sleeve, letting the gilded plate beneath gleam through the pierced foliage and flowers, animals, birds and amorini.

Chinoiserie, or decoration in the Chinese taste, has been a recurrent style in the history of English silver. Its earliest manifestation, from about 1675 to 1690, appears to have been one of the few entirely English decorative inventions. Lightly sketched and rather inaccurate palm trees, spiky foliage, and flowers provided a setting for warriors in short tunics or sages in flowing kimonos, for temples and pavilions, for exotic birds and butterflies. Cups, porringers, tankards, bowls, salvers, jars, vases and complete toilet sets were treated to this rather naive ornament.

Tea, coffee and chocolate, all of which were introduced to England about the middle of the century, quickly became fashionable. Fashionable beverages needed silverwares from which they could be served. The silversmiths' reaction was to adapt the tall flagon, making a tall, tapering, cylindrical pot with a spout and handle. It was a practical and acceptable form that soon established itself as the universal style for both coffee and chocolate, the only difference between the pots for the two drinks being the provision of a small hinged lid within the cover of the chocolate-pot through which the stirrer rod could be inserted.

The earliest known teapot (dated 1670) is in fact identical with the typical coffee-pots. It seems to have been an exception, however, and most of the earliest surviving teapots resemble small Chinese winepots, perhaps derived from porcelain or stoneware originals.

The second half of the seventeenth century saw a large rise in the consumption of both sugar and spices, and the first casters in silver date from the reign of Charles II. Here again, the straight-sided cylinder provided the basic style, with a high-domed, pierced cover held in place by sturdy bayonet clamps. Like most of the straight-sided wares of the silversmith, casters called for little decoration, and ornament was chiefly restricted to piercing, a shallow band of fluting or acanthus chasing, cut-card work or engraving.

Perhaps it was the prosperous state of life in England that made the persecuted craftsmen of France turn to this country when Louis XIV revoked the Edict of Nantes in 1685. For some years less and less toleration had been afforded to the Protestants in France, and many Huguenots did not wait for the final blow in 1685 before they fled to friendlier countries. Many of the Huguenots were craftsmen, silversmiths among them.

In 1682, Pierre Harache, an exceptionally fine craftsman, managed to break down the trade's resistance and obtained his Freedom of the Goldsmiths' Company. His was as yet a rare case of success, but he and his fellow

Frenchmen, most of them from the provinces, were soon exerting a tremendous influence on English silversmithing and laying the foundation for the supremacy of English silver during the coming century.

The Huguenot tradition was one of fine craftsmanship, sturdy gauge silver and meticulous decorative detail. They brought with them, no doubt, the design books they used in their native towns of Metz, Rouen, Poitou and so on—design books that laid emphasis on the detailed ornament known in France as *Régence*—ordered arrangements of strapwork enclosing scrolls, shells, husks and foliage, of applied lion and human head masks, of delicate cut-card and other applied work. They also brought a new variety of forms, based chiefly on the baluster shape. They introduced the cast baluster candlestick and ousted the fluted column type; they turned the straight-sided flagon into a graceful ewer with a broad high lip and flying scroll handle; they heightened the two-handled cup, making it well-proportioned and elegant with a moulded rib round the body together with a sturdy scroll or harp-shaped handles, thus ridding the silversmiths' shelves for good and all of bulging-bodied cups and coarse and ungainly embossing. Formality, simple curves and detail of design and decoration were the keynotes of Huguenot work.

From the time of the great influx of Huguenot craftsmen two distinct styles emerged—one continuing the traditions of English baroque, the other of definitely French inspiration. At times, the two merged. Silver for coffee, for instance, largely remained in the English tradition, the straight-sided, cylindrical pot with a curved spout at right angles to the scroll handle being accepted as the general style by all the silversmiths. Established, too, was the baluster cast candlestick (though the earliest ones were in fact the work of Pierre Harache in the early 1680s); with moulded, octagonal bases with sunk centres and knopped stems with cylindrical sockets, they set the style for the next half-century.

The English silversmiths seem to have remained the chief makers of some wares— perhaps understandably, since the use of silver for beer and punch drinking was typically English. Tankards remained plain and capacious; punch bowls and wine glass coolers were relics of the baroque, with fluted and gadroon-bordered panels and scalloped rims chased with cherub masks, scrolls and acanthus foliage in the most honoured baroque tradition.

At that time the Government was beginning to take a critical interest in the craft. So great was the demand for silverwares that not a few silversmiths were apparently using the coinage of the realm to make plate. In March, 1697, the Act 'for encouraging the bringing in of wrought plate to be coined' reversed the process. In addition, all new wrought silver had to be of a higher standard of fineness than sterling, which had been in force since 1300. This higher standard silver, containing 3·3 per cent more silver, was known as the *Britannia Standard* because the plate had to be marked by the assay offices with a punch showing 'the figure of a woman commonly called Britannia'.

The period of Britannia silver lasted from March, 1697, until June, 1720. Silver of this period was frequently quite plain, relying for its appeal on the beauty of line and the soft reflected mouldings. Britannia takes decoration very well and in skilled hands even better than sterling. It was merely a coincidence that much silver of the period was plain. Indeed, even after 1720 when the higher standard was no longer obligatory Paul De Lamerie, acclaimed justly as one of the greatest of all silversmiths, continued to use it for another twelve years, not even troubling to register a mark for sterling until 1732. Any implication in the wording of the Act of 1719, which restored the old sterling standard, that the new standard was too soft was probably due to the silversmiths' desire to be allowed to use the less costly sterling.

In the early years of the Britannia period, coinciding with the reign of Queen Anne, the

Huguenot styles gradually gained an ascendancy over the native ones. Probably patrons found the French designs to their liking, and the English silversmiths had perforce to follow suit.

The baluster form soon dominated most silverwares. Casters, candlesticks, jugs and teapots showed gracious curves. Coffee-pots, though mostly straight-sided, conformed with curving swan-necked spouts and scroll handles. Even some mugs and tankards appeared with tucked-in base on a circular moulded foot. The teapot of the Queen Anne period had grown away from the wine-pot style into a squat pear shape, with a high-domed cover and curved spout. Following suit was an addition to the tea-table—the tea-kettle, provided with a baluster-legged stand with a spirit lamp or charcoal brazier beneath. Only the tea-caddy stayed firmly unaffected by the baluster curve, remaining an oblong or octagonal canister, usually with a bottle-like top and sliding base. Perhaps because chocolate was more fashionable in France than in England, French styles of baluster chocolate-pot were made.

Entirely French in conception, and almost always made by French silversmiths in England, were helmet-shaped jugs and ewers. Differing considerably in decorative detail, they were generally of similar form; mounted on a circular, moulded foot, the body was divided by two ribs; the upper one followed the outline of the rim and spout and usually featured an applied mask or other decoration immediately below the spout; the flying-scroll handle was sometimes cast as an arching caryatid. The bases were usually, though not invariably, enriched with applied work.

Applied detail and engraving were the two great decorative treatments of the Queen Anne period. Though much domestic silver was relatively plain, few important 'state' pieces were left unadorned. At the turn of the century there was a revival and a refinement of cut-card ornament. Delicate and detailed cut-out designs, sometimes enhanced with chasing, were applied round the bases of

A small coffee-pot by Charles Kandler. The fluted body is richly chased and the spout capped with a leaf motif; the handle is wood.
Ashmolean Museum.

cups, ewers, bowls, pilgrim flasks (the great wine bottles used for cooling wine), coffee-pots, teapots, tankards, jugs and the tops of casters. Cast applied detail was another Huguenot trait soon adopted by all competent silversmiths.

Engraving on silver was of an exceptionally high order during the reigns of William III, Queen Anne and George I, and a number of very beautiful salvers and dishes have survived. In contrast, some salvers and waiters were plain, or decorated no more than with a moulded or gadrooned rim and an engraved coat-of-arms or crest. Variety was sometimes achieved by the form only—square, circular, octagonal, hexagonal or multi-lobed. Shallow dishes with fluted edges, known as strawberry dishes, were made in various sizes from small saucer types to large bowls, some nine or ten inches in diameter. These too, might be left plain, or delicately chased or engraved within each of the flutes.

The reign of George I saw the new age of the dining service. Plates and dishes in silver were nothing new, but now there were also soup tureens, sauce boats, and knives, forks and spoons made *en suite*. Forks in England had been rather late arrivals (those made prior to 1690 being very rare indeed). They were, however, included among the dinner-table wares of the early eighteenth-century home. About the turn of the seventeenth century, the trifid end of spoons and forks became rounded off to the shield top, with a flattened stem and a rat-tail down the back of the spoon-bowl. Forks were sometimes two-pronged, usually three-pronged. During the reign of Queen Anne, the shield top was replaced by the round end, known as Hanoverian, but still with a plain rat-tail. Hanoverian remained the favourite pattern of flatware until superseded by Old English in the later eighteenth century and by more decorative patterns during the Regency.

Rococo was of French origin. It probably takes its strange name from *rocaille*, and was, indeed, a fantasy of rocks and marine creatures, flowers and shells and scrolls, leaping dolphins and foliate fronds.

About 1750 there was another revival of chinoiserie, this time executed in repoussé chased designs and in pierced work. It was an aptly popular fashion for all kinds of tea-table silver. Many a caddy and sugar-box was chased with robed figures, oriental flowers and gabled houses in the Chinese taste. As often as not, the chinoiserie designs were inextricably mixed with the scrolls and shells of the rococo.

During the 1760s pagoda-like roofs, Chinese figures and temple bells appeared on the elaborately pierced basket épergnes used as table centrepieces on formal occasions. The bridges, coolie figures, palm trees and strange plants associated by the English silversmiths with Chinese art were used with considerable delicacy for the pierced baskets and épergne stands as a contrast to the cherub-mounted, scrolling branches and shell- and flower-crusted rococo épergnes. Even pierced salts with cut-glass bowls were made in that style about 1760.

By the 1760s, even the most eager rococo-ists were tiring of asymmetry. Some silversmiths tended to look again across the Channel and to formalise silver in the French manner once more. Tureens were made shallower, with wavy rims and finials in the form of fruit or vegetables, rather like those made in porcelain. Sometimes ripple-fluted effects were achieved. On occasion, perhaps fostered by Sir Horace Walpole's Strawberry Hill home, there was silver made in the Gothic style. The silver of the late 1750s and the 1760s was silver in a transitional style.

For several years London society had been eloquently discussing and avidly following the excavations of classical sites at Palmyra, Baalbek, Rome and Herculaneum. Artists and architects visited the sites for themselves, and returned with sketches and scale drawings and plenty of ideas to put into practice. Among them was the young Scottish architect, Robert Adam. The acknowledged aim of the neo-classicists was to draw on 'the most elegant ornament of the most refined Grecian articles'. Laurel wreaths and festoons, anthemion, palmette and scroll borders were neat and restrained after the contorted cult of rococoism. The stone urn and the vase provided an elegant new shape for silver—so few metal-wares had been uncovered in the excavations anyway.

A development of engraving called bright-cut was particularly suited to the Adam designs that soon came to be made in silver. Fluting was equally suitable for echoing the slender marble pillars and pilasters beloved of Adam, and it was also well suited to the new stamping processes which were being used, especially in Sheffield, for making candlesticks.

The very simplicity of the vase and the oval made them suitable for domestic silver such as teapots, tea urns, sugar bowls and swing-handled baskets, soup and sauce tureens as well as for the ubiquitous cups and covers that were presented as race trophies and on every possible civic occasion as well. The classical column was tapered, and topped with an urn finial for candlesticks and candelabra. Beading and reeding were the most favoured border ornaments. Piercing was as restrained as the regular galleried frets of Chinese Chippendale, though the épergne makers, now constrained by the oval and formal classical motifs, did achieve scroll and leaf-pierced borders, and added interest to pierced boat-shapes by using deep-blue glass liners.

The success of Adam and the neo-classicists lay in their elegant, delicate designs, but Wyatt and Henry Holland had more grandiose tendencies, while by 1800 even the King voiced an opinion that 'the Adams have introduced too much of neatness and prettiness'. In silver, however, the 'sippets of embroidery' had already started to give way to a grander style by the 1790's. There was more pronounced and even applied decoration overlaying the simplicity of the Grecian. Festoons, once only bright-cut, were now chased with a Roman majesty; small applied medallions, modelled of course on classical lines, were used particularly by Fogelburg and Gilbert on jugs and teapots. Lion masks once again appeared at the knuckles of sauce boats and footed tureens; bold leafage, ovolos and scrolls in relief, and reed and tie borders began to supersede beading and simple reeding. Once again, the tide of taste was changing, and sweeping in with the tide, urging it fast ahead, was the Prince of Wales, the last and most powerful of all the great dilettanti.

'Prinny' was an enthusiastic and a lavish patron, though his genius and taste were not always either elegant or wise. He had grandiose schemes for building and furnishing, but changed his mind with infuriating regularity. In Rundell & Bridge he found an ambitious firm of goldsmiths who were ready to cater to his strangest whim. They commissioned artists and sculptors to produce designs for plate. Now all sign of Adam grace vanished. 'Massiveness', boomed C. H. Tatham, 'is the principal characteristic of good Plate,' and 'good Chasing . . . a branch of Sculpture.' At Rundell & Bridge's behest men such as Tatham, John Flaxman and Stothard turned the silversmith into a vehicle for producing sculpture in silver.

A most distressing habit, in the eyes of the modern collector at any rate, was the 'improving' of old pieces of plain silver by the addition of a revived rococo chasing. This was not only a Victorian weakness, and there are records both of added decoration and alterations made in the period between 1818 and 1830. It was not a practice intended to defraud, but merely to conform to fashion.

Machines were also being put to work. In Birmingham and Sheffield in particular stamping presses were turning out copies of fashionable silver. For quite a long time, the machine-made products were reasonably well designed. They were often copies of handmade pieces. Sheffield candlesticks were, indeed, good examples of silver made by stamping in sections, assembly and loading. It was later, mostly in the 1830s and after, that there was the temptation to use a base from here, a stem from there, a socket from another design.

The London silversmiths were still, on the whole, hand craftsmen, but they, too, were caught in the net of grandiosity for its own sake. Storr and Smith, who both survived the Regency by many years, were masters of their craft and essayed many pieces—especially after both had broken with Rundell & Bridge—that hinted at the trends the craft might have taken if the silversmiths had been left on their own. Their virtuosity ranged over every style—from noble Roman and elegant Greek to an almost modern simplicity of curves and plain surfaces.

Sheffield Plate was introduced as a substitute for silver and to provide a wider public with pleasant and decorative wares. In 1840 the invention of electroplating meant yet another commodity with which silver had to compete. The early Victorian period, with its huge industrial upheavals, its quickly rich and its multiplying poor, changed the face of Britain. The Victorians did not, however, stifle craftsmanship. They extolled it. Two years before Queen Victoria came to the throne, a 'Select Committee on Arts and

SILVER

Manufactures' was appointed by Parliament. It strongly recommended forging links between fine and applied arts and industrial production. 'It equally imports us to encourage art in its loftier attributes,' the committee sententiously reported, 'since it is admitted that the cultivation of the more exalted branches of design tends to advance the humblest pursuits of industry.' But even in 1835, it was almost too late. No exhibition, no laboured patronage, could reassemble the shattered fabric of a broken tradition, in which neither design nor craftsmanship followed their original courses.

Below and on the following page is the complete list of assay-office marks from 1638–1916 of the London date letters; full cycles existed before, but the great periods of English silver followed the Restoration. At the head of each column are the appropriate London assay-office marks which have changed with each new cycle. The last column on page 41 gives the main provincial marks.

Cycle 1	Cycle 2	Cycle 3	Cycle 4	Cycle 5	Cycle 6	Cycle 7	Cycle 8
1638-9	1658-9	1678-9	MAR to MAY 1697	1716-7	1736-7	1756-7	177
1639-0	1659-0	1679-0	1697-8	1717-8	1737-8	1757-8	177
1640-1	1660-1	1680-1	1698-9	1718-9	1738-9	1758-9	177
1641-2	1661-2	1681-2	1699-0	1719-0	1739-0	1759-0	177
1642-3	1662-3	1682-3	1700-1	1720-1	1740-1	1760-1	178
1643-4	1663-4	1683-4	1701-2	1721-2	1741-2	1761-2	178
1644-5	1664-5	1684-5	1702-3	1722-3	1742-3	1762-3	178
1645-6	1665-6	1685-6	1703-4	1723-4	1743-4	1763-4	178
1646-7	1666-7	1686-7	1704-5	1724-5	1744-5	1764-5	178
1647-8	1667-8	1687-8	1705-6	1725-6	1745-6	1765-6	178
1648-9	1668-9	1688-9	1706-7	1726-7	1746-7	1766-7	178
1649-0	1669-0	1689-0	1707-8	1727-8	1747-8	1767-8	178
1650-1	1670-1	1690-1	1708-9	1728-9	1748-9	1768-9	178
1651-2	1671-2	1691-2	1709-0	1729-0	1749-0	1769-0	178
1652-3	1672-3	1692-3	1710-1	1730-1	1750-1	1770-1	179
1653-4	1673-4	1693-4	1711-2	1731-2	1751-2	1771-2	179
1654-5	1674-5	1694-5	1712-3	1732-3	1752-3	1772-3	179
1655-6	1675-6	1695-6	1713-4	1733-4	1753-4	1773-4	179
1656-7	1676-7	30 MAY 1696 TO MAR 1697	1714-5	1734-5	1754-5	1774-5	179
1657-8	1677-8	NO LETTER	1715-6	1735-6	1755-6	1775-6	179

a. from June, 1720   b. from i

40

												Provincial Marks
	1796-7	**a**	1816-7	𝕬	1836-7	𝖆	1856-7	A	1876-7	**a**	1896-7	ENGLAND
	1797-8	**b**	1817-8	𝕭	1837-8	𝖇	1857-8	B	1877-8	**b**	1897-8	⚓ Birmingham
	1798-9	**c**	1818-9	𝕮	1838-9	𝖈	1858-9	C	1878-9	**c**	1898-9	👑 Sheffield
	1799-0	**d**	1819-0	𝕯	1839-0	𝖉	1859-0	D	1879-0	**d**	1899-0	Chester
	1800-1	**e**	1820-1	𝕰	1840-1	𝖊	1860-1	E	1880-1	**e**	1900-1	Exeter
	1801-2	**f**	1821-2	𝕱	1841-2	𝖋	1861-2	F	1881-2	**f**	1901-2	Newcastle
	1802-3	**g**	1822-3	𝕲	1842-3	𝖌	1862-3	G	1882-3	**g**	1902-3	Norwich
	1803-4	**h**	1823-4	𝕳	1843-4	𝖍	1863-4	H	1883-4	**h**	1903-4	York
	1804-5	**i**	1824-5	𝕴	1844-5	𝖎	1864-5	I	1884-5	**i**	1904-5	Hull
	1805-6	**k**	1825-6	𝕶	1845-6	𝖐	1865-6	K	1885-6	**k**	1905-6	Bristol
	1806-7	**l**	1826-7	𝕷	1846-7	𝖑	1866-7	L	1886-7	**l**	1906-7	
	1807-8	**m**	1827-8	𝕸	1847-8	𝖒	1867-8	M	1887-8	**m**	1907-8	
	1808-9	**n**	1828-9	𝕹	1848-9	𝖓	1868-9	N	1888-9	**n**	1908-9	
	1809-0	**o**	1829-0	𝕺	1849-0	𝖔	1869-0	O	1889-0	**o**	1909-0	
	1810-1	**p**	1830-1	𝕻	1850-1	𝖕	1870-1	P	1890-1	**p**	1910-1	
	1811-2	**q**	1831-2	𝕼	1851-2	𝖖	1871-2	Q	1891-2	**q**	1911-2	
	1812-3	**r**	1832-3	𝕽	1852-3	𝖗	1872-3	R	1892-3	**r**	1912-3	
	1813-4	**s**	1833-4	𝕾	1853-4	𝖘	1873-4	S	1893-4	**s**	1913-4	
	1814-5	**t**	1834-5	𝕿	1854-5	𝖙	1874-5	T	1894-5	**t**	1914-5	
	1815-6	**u**	1835-6	𝖀	1855-6	𝖚	1875-6	U	1895-6	**u**	1915-6	

om 1821

d. from 1837

e. Queen Victoria duty mark to 1890

A plain-body tankard of the Charles II type. It was made in 1661; the maker used an 'Orb and cross' marking. Note the position of the hallmarks.
Garrard & Co. Ltd.

A porringer and cover made in 1663; the cover by the same maker dates from 1661. It is repoussé chased with a goat on one side and a lion on the other.
Christie, Manson and Woods Ltd.

42

A caster made in 1690 by Pierre Harache, the first Huguenot silversmith to be admitted to the Freedom of the Goldsmiths' Company. It marks the introduction of that refinement in ornament and decoration which characterises the work of the Huguenots.

Mrs. N. B. Munro

A pair of baluster candlesticks made by Ralph Leeke in 1690. They follow the designs of Pierre Harache and were made with little variation until 1718.

Biggs of Maidenhead Ltd.

43

Left: *a cup and cover made by Pierre Platel, the teacher of Paul De Lamerie, in 1702. It represents the undoubted quality of design and craftsmanship of Huguenot work.* Right: *a conical
coffee-pot made by Andrew Raven in 1700. Note the cut-card work around the handle sockets.*
Ashmolean Museum.

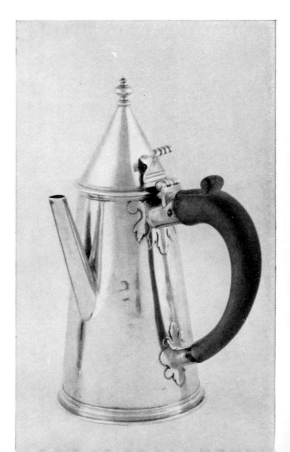

A punch bowl made by Isaac Dighton in 1699. It is now at Temple Newsam House near Leeds.

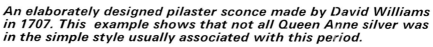

An elaborately designed pilaster sconce made by David Williams in 1707. This example shows that not all Queen Anne silver was in the simple style usually associated with this period.

Victoria & Albert Museum.

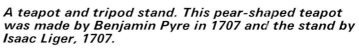

A teapot and tripod stand. This pear-shaped teapot was made by Benjamin Pyre in 1707 and the stand by Isaac Liger, 1707.

S. J. Shrubsole Ltd.

Heavy-gauge silver sauce-boats from the workshop of Sarah Holaday and made in 1721.

One of a set of four salts made by Paul De Lamerie in 1731. Note the lion mark and paw decoration.

Left: *a trio of casters made by Edmund Pearce in 1720.*
Right: *a sugar bowl made by William Fordham in 1730.*
Sotheby & Co. and W. H. Willson Ltd.

Two baskets made by Paul De Lamerie in 1734.
Thomas Lumley Ltd.

A small ewer made by Crespin in
1727. Note the simple 'spoon
handle' straps below and the rich
rococo feeling of the upper half.
Ashmolean Museum.

A pair of bottle-top tea canisters
made in 1726. The only decoration
is limited to the owner's
coat-of-arms.
Thomas Lumley Ltd.

A simple teapot with engraved
coat-of-arms and foliate
decoration. Made by
Gabriel Sleath in 1733.

An inkstand on four scroll feet and made by William Cripps in 1747.

S. J. Shrubsole Ltd.

A pair of tumbler cups made by Thomas Whipham and Charles Wright in 1767. These cups had a heavy base so that they would return to up-right if tipped off centre.

Mrs. W. B. Munro.

An elaborate centrepiece of 'épergne' by Thomas Pitts and made in 1763. Note the four sets of candle branches.

Christie, Manson & Woods Ltd.

One of a pair of fine cruets made by Richard Bayley in 1740 for the Worshipful Company of Goldsmiths.
Garrard & Co. Ltd.

A soup tureen and stand made by Paul Crespin in 1740. It is one of the most remarkable and exotic pieces ever made in England. It is in the rococo style and is 21¾ inches overall and weighs 524 ozs.

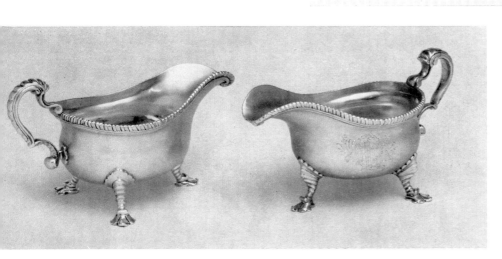

Two sauce boats made by Daniel Piers in 1749. Note the 'quilted' decoration on the feet and the double-scroll handles.
Spink & Son Ltd.

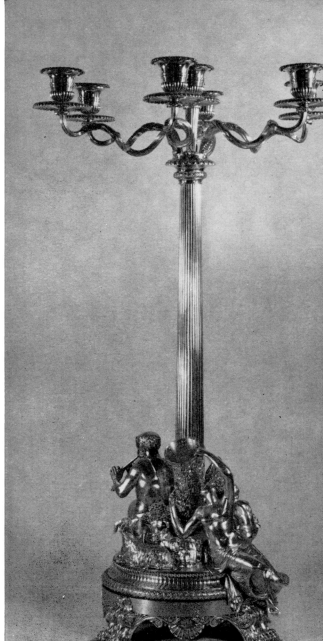

This magnificent candelabrum was made in 1814 by Paul Storr, probably the best-known of all Regency silversmiths. The beautiful base is a group of Pan, nymphs and goats. It stands 37 inches high.
Worshipful Company of Goldsmiths.

A wine cooler, one of a pair made by Daniel Smith and Robert Sharp in 1804. Note the finely modelled heads of Perseus below the serpent handles.

Thomas Lumley Ltd.

A large tray (23 inches wide) made by John Crouch and Thomas Hannam in 1793.

Christie, Manson & Woods Ltd.

A set of four silver-gilt decanter stands made by William Burwash in 1817.
Thomas Lumley Ltd.

A silver-gilt cake basket made by J. & E. Terry in 1820.
Thomas Lumley Ltd.

A cruet stand made by Robert
Harper in 1874. It has scroll-
pierced sides, cast scroll feet and
a shell handle. It contains six blue
glass bottles for condiments
and sauces.

A magnificent example of the later
work of Paul Storr. This dessert
dish is one of a set of four made in
1838.

Christie, Manson & Woods Ltd.

Paul Sandby
1725–1809
An ancient beech tree.

WATERCOLOURS

It has been said that the watercolour is a peculiarly English art. This is to claim too much, for watercolour neither began in England, nor did it develop here independent of foreign influences. Dürer made extensive and effective use of watercolour on landscape, figure and topographical drawings. The early English topographical watercolourists were extensively influenced by the art of the Low Countries and Central Europe; the early English landscape watercolourists by the Italians. What can be said, however, is that from the mid eighteenth to the mid nineteenth century there existed in England such a constellation of talented watercolourists as had never been seen in one country before, whose output, in spite of great varieties in style, techniques and subject-matter, gave a distinct English flavour to the art.

The tradition of English watercolourists began in the 16th century, and one of the earliest practitioners was John White, who sailed with Raleigh to America in 1585 and illustrated the life of the American Indians. But in this short introduction we will concern ourselves primarily with the eighteenth and nineteenth century, during which period the talents and the output of the English watercolourists were at their most intense. The twentieth century, too, has seen a great deal of talented work in the medium, but this, of necessity, we must ignore. We have already had to be highly selective in our choice of earlier artists; one could not do the same with artists who are still at work, and whose art is still being weighed and assessed, without making serious mistakes.

We may begin with Paul Sandby and Alexander Cozens, though to do so is to skip over many talented artists—Van Dyke, Inigo Jones, the panoramic scenes of Wenceslaus Hollar, the coast scenes, towns and ruins of Francis Place, and naturalist artists of the early eighteenth century, and the romantic landscapes of William Taverner. Nevertheless, Sandby and Cozens are convenient figures to start with because they stand at the head of the two chief groups of eighteenth century watercolour artists: the topographical—reliable representations of views in town and country—and the landscape—the imaginative rearrangement of the same materials into an aesthetic composition.

Paul Sandby (1730–1809) was not exclusively a topographer, but he did a great deal of this kind of work, and he was certainly one of the first artists to draw attention to the remote beauties of Wales and Scotland, and to popularise them by means of aquatints. He was attracted, too, by delapidated ruins as well as refined architectural views. It seems unlikely that he did much purely imaginative work, but apart from topography, he did some fine studies, notably of trees. Incidentally, Sandby used both clear and opaque colour. Opaque colour (it may be body colour, gouache, tempera or distemper) is the oldest kind of watercolour and was the kind used on medieval MSS. The lights are produced by mixing an opaque white pigment with the colours, while in 'clear' watercolour the lights are produced by the lightness of the paper shining through the transparent washes of colour. The two processes may be used together, but over-use of opaque colour deprives a watercolour of its distinctive character and makes it more like an oil, and may encourage the introduction of excessive detail, a fault of many Victorian watercolour paintings.

Alexander Cozens (1717–1768), on the other hand, generally painted what he saw in his mind, though his 'props' and characters were drawn from nature. He took nature and rearranged it. He is a vital figure in the development of the English landscape watercolour, yet not because of his colour, for indeed he hardly ever used any, his most characteristic medium being the brown wash. His great contribution was just this: that he was able, without colour, to produce a landscape that was 'luminous' and grand, that faded into invisible distance, that, like a wide-angled lens, took in great breadth and impressive height at one sweep. Cozens was also a great protagonist of systems, above all the method of 'blot-drawing' which enabled him, and his pupils, to concentrate on the composition of a painting first and the details later. By means of full brush and broad strokes in all directions, he would represent a general idea on a piece of paper, such as a ruin on a hill. He would then put tracing paper over this 'blot' and use the broad strokes to suggest the smaller features of the picture, which would thus fit in with the general composition.

Both of these men had their followers. The topographical tradition was continued by such men as Thomas Hearne, Joseph Farringdon and Thomas Daniell. Among landscape artists there was perhaps greater individuality, for the medium encouraged it. Direct influences are less easy to trace; indirect ones are legion. Thomas Gainsborough (1728–1788) was one of the greatest figures in eighteenth-century landscape art, yet, like Cozens, he usually confined himself to monochrome washes, and his watercolour style was hardly distinguishable from his style in

other mediums. This style varies from the close approximations to nature of his early period in Suffolk to his style at Bath, and later, when he would construct landscapes on his table at home by means of stones and pieces of herbs and would interpret them into a landscape by candlelight.

Some wide-ranging spirits dabbled in watercolour as a diversion from their usual pursuits. Robert Adam (1728–1792) produced, in the 1770s and 1780s, some unlikely watercolours of unlikely romantic landscapes and buildings, such as castles on improbably steep-sided hills. It was customary, of course, for architects to colour their drawings with watercolours.

Constable was gracious enough to say that John Robert Cozens (1752–1797) son of Alexander, was 'the greatest genius that ever touched landscape'. He was one of a generation of artists who were powerfully influenced by touring on the Continent, especially in Italy, and it is on his landscapes of Switzerland, Italy and the Tyrol that his reputation is based. He toured the Continent twice, the second time with William Beckford. His later life is obscure, and he produced very few drawings while he was in England. He became insane in 1794 and was looked after by Dr. Thomas Monro, a great patron of artists at the end of the century, and a watercolourist in his own right. J. R. Cozens' range of colour was small—though wider than his father's—mainly grey and blue, fawn and dark green. Yet, like his father, he had a magnificent sense of height and distance and the fine composition of imposing views.

Francis Towne (1739–1816) painted in a quite different and highly original style. He incorporated into the rather formalised design of his drawings, shapes and patterns of flat colour which Iolo Williams has suggested had a marked affinity to the Japanese coloured wood-engravings. His visits to the Italian Alps in 1780 and 1781 brought his style to its artistic peak, though he had done fine work in Wales in 1777 and was to do more in the Lake District in 1786. In the Alps he was less restrained in his use of colour, and used bold designs simplified to the last degree with occasional touches of highly effective detail.

Apart from the topographical and landscape artists of the eighteenth century, there was also a group of artists who were more concerned with figure draughtsmanship, some as book illustrators, some as social satirists, some because only through figures could they express the full intensity of their feelings. Head-and-shoulders above the rest in this group stand Blake and Rowlandson.

William Blake (1757–1827) sometimes combined the print and the watercolour, but where he only used pen and watercolour his pictures are generally rather less forceful than his engravings, though they are quite as formal in design and the subject-matter is of the same kind. Generally, he did not use strong colour, and it might be said that in many of his watercolours the picture is essentially complete before the colour is applied, being in essence a design built up from the sinuous lines of the human body. *The Wise and Foolish Virgins* is a good example of this. But occasionally he used strong colour with great effect, as in the pinnacles of blue and red flames, contrasting with the soft red and blue clothes of Dante and his guide, to be found in *The Inscription over Hell Gate*.

Thomas Rowlandson (1756–1827) was a quite different character from the prophet and poet Blake, being primarily, though not exclusively, a social satirist. A Rowlandson figure subject, even a portrait, is not so much a character as the distilled essence of the social group that he had chosen to portray. Once this limitation is accepted, he must be admitted to the ranks of the great and original watercolourists. An outstanding example is *Old Vauxhall Gardens* in which a microcosm of the London scene in the late eighteenth century—the court, the literati, the stage—is revealed among the trees and architecture (both strongly drawn with the brush) of the gardens. The caricature is restrained, and the stances and attitudes are perfect, rapidly conveying the easy-going joviality of the occasion. Rowlandson could also be effective in his portrayal of animals, especially dogs, though his landscapes are sometimes rather dull unless peopled with the figures that were his great strength.

At the turn of the century, two figures are outstanding among watercolour artists, though one had not yet reached his maturity and the other was to die tragically young. They were J. M. W. Turner and Thomas Girtin (1775–1802). Their early careers were closely connected. Girtin was at first taught by Edward Dayes, but they disagreed and parted, and Girtin early made friends with Turner. For three years they did copying work together at Dr. Monro's house for a small salary. Girtin also belonged to a sketching club known as 'the Brothers'. Almost all of his important work comes in the last six years of his life. In Paris and London he began to produce the architectural watercolours in which he was able to convey the masses, shapes and colouring of buildings without cluttering and painting with unnecessary architectural details. But it was in landscape that he was at his best, and some regard him as the greatest watercolourist in this field. We have mentioned the talents of other artists for depth and width in their paintings. Girtin is able to suggest an immense width of vision 'on a few square inches of paper'. The main features of his landscapes cross the painting in magnificent sweeps, while the details are few and telling —the occasional figure, an animal, a windmill or barn.

J. M. W. Turner (1775–1851) passed through a number of artistic phases, and people strongly disagree as to when he was at the height of his powers. Early on in his career, at the time that he painted *Tintern Abbey*, his work is part of the tradition of the picturesque topographers of the 18th century. Later, he is a 19th century romantic and shows the influence of Constable, and later still he is concerned primarily with colour and only the impression of a subject is attempted. Perhaps his finest work in watercolour was done during his last visit to Venice and at Petworth. How strongly he relied on colour in those Venetian subjects can be seen by examining black-and-white reproductions of the paintings. They seem hardly to exist except as faint, grey shadows. Only an occasional feature such as a ship or a gondola is drawn with any strength at all. Yet, in his luminous colour, they make a deep impression of the etherealised scene he imagined. The subject-matter was quite different at Petworth, for Turner concentrated mainly on the interior of the house, yet it is the same aspects—colour, light and shade—on which he concentrates: there is light filtering through a window, the flickering light of a fire, the light of the lamps.

We have seen how the landscapes of Scotland, Wales, and later Italy, exercised a profound effect on the watercolourists of the 18th century. At the turn of the century a new breed of artists was drawing inspiration from East Anglia; some, like Constable, from Suffolk and Essex, others—and this is a much larger group—from Norfolk. The latter made up the Norwich School, which developed, it has been suggested, because Norwich was very much more isolated from London than other provincial centres, and because there was so much talent there at the same time that the artists had no need to feel cut off from fellow-practitioners. The leading lights of the School were John Crome and John Sell Cotman. John Crome (1768–1821) painted few watercolours, yet those few are enough to entitle him to be called a great watercolourist.

John Sell Cotman (1782–1848) was not exclusively a Norwich artist. He came under the influence of Girtin in his early career, perhaps when he worked at Dr. Monro's house (though Girtin was no longer there) and later through 'the Brothers'; and he also sought inspiration in Yorkshire and Normandy. But he always remained attached to Norwich and was a member of the Society. As his mature style developed, he began to use bold areas of flat pattern—as we have mentioned Towne had done, but in a quite

different manner. In *Chirk Aqueduct*, for example, a bold, whitish pattern is made by the arches of the aqueduct that completely dominate the picture, and are repeated again as a reflection in the water. The wooded valley behind the arches is in his characteristic subdued greens, and the sky and water are in soft blues and greys. But Yorkshire was Cotman's greatest source of inspiration, and it was here, between 1803 and 1805, that he produced his finest work, and it remained in his mind for a long while afterwards. *Greta Bridge*, painted shortly after he left Yorkshire, again makes use of a whitish bridge—this time a broad-spanned bridge—as the central part of the design. A plain stone house stands at one end of the bridge, while at the other side there are clumps of brownish trees. The river below the bridge widens out into a broad, calm pool before it breaks over rocks in a white foam. The greyish sky is largely obscured by brilliant white clouds.

John Constable (1776–1837) was primarily an oil painter, and his work in watercolours is a small and incidental part of his main output. He did some large watercolours, such as *Old Sarum* and *Stonehenge*, and many brilliant smaller sketches—pencil and watercolour figure drawings and studies of trees, and, perhaps his finest achievement, studies in clouds.

David Cox and Peter De Wint cover almost exactly the same period, and were regarded in the mid-nineteenth century as the classic exponents of the medium. Both were influenced by John Varley (1778–1842) who also taught Cox, but they found their inspiration in different places—Cox in Wales, De Wint in Lincoln and the valleys of the Trent and Thames.

David Cox (1783–1859) produced pictures of varying artistic merit, yet there are fine pictures from all periods of his life, though there are more from the later period when he had determinedly broken away from the excessive prettiness of some of his earlier work. It was the countryside in and around Bettwys-y-Coed, that pleased him most, and it is in the blustery Welsh landscapes that he is most successful, and among the wild moorlands, rocks and mountains.

Peter De Wint (1784–1849), on the other hand, was principally inclined towards pastoral and riverside subjects: corn stooks, village scenes, horses and carts and barges. He was also fond of still life studies and architectural subjects. His great strength was colour: deep, rich tones. But he was not always successful even as a colourist, perhaps because his palette was rather limited.

Like Girtin, R. P. Bonington (1802–1828) died tragically young. His work was by no means exclusively English, for he spent much time in France and was greatly influenced by Delacroix. Yet it was he who popularised the English watercolour in France, with his seascapes, architectural studies and views of Venice. His great quality was his sense of light and colour. He perhaps appreciated the moods of sunlight as no one else had done before him.

Samuel Palmer (1805–1881) was influenced by John Linnell and by Blake. Unlike the latter, Palmer 'clung to the earth', but he followed Blake in isolating himself from the influence of his contemporaries and produced a highly independent style. This he developed in the seclusion of his 'valley of vision' at Shoreham in Kent, and here he produced his most striking work. 'Excess is the essential vivyfying spirit, vital spark, embalming spice . . . of the finest art', he wrote. This, together with the beauty of his surroundings and his profound love of the countryside are all one needs to explain the extraordinary quality of his paintings.

The artists detailed above are among the most outstanding English watercolour artists but there are quite a few more of above average talent whose work is well worth collecting. It is impossible to detail the work of all of them here, but the work of the following, arranged alphabetically, is recommended; Thomas Barker (1769–1847), known as Barker of Bath, William Callow (1812–1908), George Cattermole (1800–1868), Joshua Cristall (1767–1847), Edward Duncan (1803–1882), Myles Birket Foster (1825–1899), William Havell (1782–1857), Thomas Hearne (1744–1817), James Holland (1800–1870), William Henry Hunt (1790–1864), Edward Lear (1812–1888), John Mogford (1821–1885), Samuel Prout (1783–1852), J. B. Pyne (1800–1870), William Turner (1789–1862), Thomas Uwins (1782–1857), John Varley (1778–1842), William Westall (1781–1850), Edmund Wimperis (1835–1900).

David Cox
1783–1859
The Llug Meadows
near Hereford.

Peter de Wint
1784–1849
View from Gore Lane,
Kensington, showing
St. Luke's Church, Chelsea.

Richard Parkes Bonington
1802–1828
French coast with
fishing boats.

Thomas Gainsborough
1727–1788
Landscape with
archway of rock.

ohn Sell Cotman
782–1842
Vindmill in Lincolnshire.

Francis Towne
1740–1816
Part of Ambleside
at the head of the
lake of Windermere.

William Henry Pyne
1769–1843
Fishermen's houses
by the Thames.

John Robert Cozens
1752–1797
Shepherd's hut.

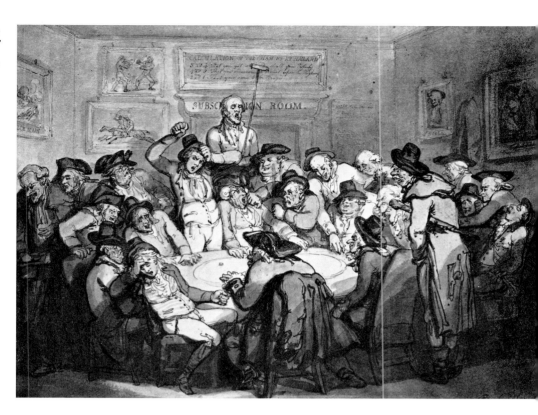

Thomas Rowlandson
1756–1827
The Hazard Room.

William Blake
1757–1827
St. Augustine and
the British captives.

William Daniell
1769–1837
Durham Cathedral.

Edward Lear
1812–1888
Cedars of Lebanon.

Frederick Goodall
1822–1904
The children of Charles I.

64

William Leighton Leitch
1804–1883
The town and castle of
Dumbarton from the river Leven.

Myles Birket Foster
1825–1899
Children playing.

Samuel Palmer
1805–1881
Tintern Abbey.

All photographs in this section
are reproduced by courtesy of
the Victoria and Albert Museum.

Late seventeenth century dwarf ale glasses of lead metal and rather heavy gadrooning.
(Sydney Crompton)

A large rummer made about 1685. It has a hollow cylindrical stem decorated with six raspberry punts in relief.
Corning Museum of Glass.

GLASS

The English glass industry is still comparatively young; good-quality table glass has only been produced in England since the end of the fifteenth century. We may compare this with the industry in Egypt, which was established by 1370 B.C. or with that of Rome, which already held the secret of most of the methods of hand production and decoration that we know today. It is true that in the late middle ages window-glass and rough glass vessels were being produced in England, but the work was primarily in the hands of foreigners and cannot be compared with the glasses which the Venetians were producing at the same time, whose delicacy and complex decoration even the Victorians had to struggle to reproduce. Yet, for two reasons, English glass occupies an important place in any history of glass production.

In the first place, it was in England that 'lead' glass was first produced successfully and on a large scale. This was the result of the work of George Ravenscroft (1618–1681) who, for the first time, obtained the silica needed for glassmaking from English instead of Venetian flints and added an oxide of lead called litharge. His glass was heavier than the Venetian glass, but superior in its brilliance and its remarkable light-dispersing quality. The simple and elegant designs of

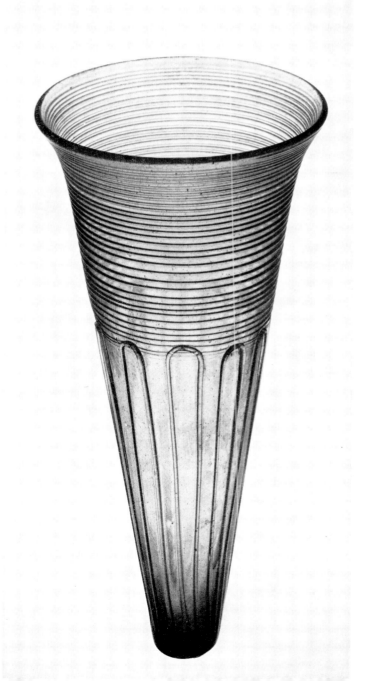

An Anglo-Saxon beaker of free-blown olive-green glass. It is post-Roman, fifth century, A.D.
Corning Museum of Glass

the end of the seventeenth century and the first half of the eighteenth century showed the glass off at its best, and the work of George Ravenscroft and the glassmakers who succeeded him not only produced the first authentically English style in glasses but also reached the high-water mark of English glass production for all time. For the second reason we must look to the mid-nineteenth century, when, throughout Europe as well as in England, glasses were being produced that were little more than a hotchpot of ancient techniques and the designs of earlier periods, technically brilliant but aesthetically worthless. William Morris reacted against this, as he reacted against heavy Victorian furniture

and repressive Victorian social conditions, by trying to start again from first principles. In 1859, he commissioned his friend Philip Webb to design some wineglasses and tumblers for him in simple, elegant shapes, and this marked the beginning of a revival of handmade blown glass, taking its inspiration from Roman and Medieval glass. Fine glass production in the twentieth century, both in Europe and America, has followed on from this.

Collectors are no longer likely to come across glasses produced in England before Ravenscroft's time, and would probably not recognize them as such if they did, for they were produced by continental craftsmen in a

A glass made at the factory run by Jacopo Verzelini in London. The bowl is decorated with the arms of the Vintner's Company and bears the date 1590.

Sidney Crompton.

style barely distinguishable from that of Venice or of l'Altare in Montferrat. Most of the examples that have been identified are in museums, and, if they came on to the market, would be extremely expensive. Few collectors go further back than the period of the baluster stem glasses (roughly 1675 to 1720). At first these had solid baluster or inverted baluster stems beneath a round funnel or V-shaped bowl, and were otherwise plain; but later the glassmakers began to embellish them with 'knops' of all shapes and sizes, drop knops, annulated knops, cushioned knops, acorn knops, egg knops, mushroom knops, and many more. The bowls often had thick, solid bases, sometimes with a tear in them, and the usual shapes were the conical, the round funnel and the waisted.

Immediately after the accession of George I in 1714, a style appeared in England derived from the glasses of Hesse and west Germany, which we call Silesian. It featured a moulded pedestal stem which was ribbed and shouldered, four-sided at first but later, and more commonly, eight sided. The style was also used for tapersticks, candlesticks and sweetmeat glasses.

By the 1720s the heavy baluster glasses in high quality metal were being replaced by a lighter style, for the manufacturers wished to make cheaper glasses that could be sold to a wider public. Thus began the period of the balustroid stem (1725–50). Glasses now had smaller bowls and longer stems. The 'Kitcat' glasses, named after a type which Kneller depicted the Kitcat Club using to drink a toast, were typical. They had a trumpet bowl on a baluster stem, with a plain section beneath, and sometimes a base knop. The light baluster or Newcastle glasses (1735–65) were of a better quality than the balustroids, and, with their tall, slender, knopped stems, are some of the most elegant glasses produced. Newcastle was a very important glassmaking centre at this time, and its products were in heavy demand not only in England but also on the continent as they were better material for the engraver than

Left: *wineglass with a conical bowl and* **right:** *with ovoid bowl. Both made about 1710.*
Dr. D. L. Mackenzie.

the continental potash-lime glasses. The largest group of glasses made between 1740 and 1770 had plain straight stems, and were turned out cheaply and in large quantities for the popular market. Though not as attractive as those we have already mentioned, some of them are well proportioned and many engraved with patriotic slogans or hop and barley motifs. Some dram glasses have a heavy 'firing' foot: when club-members wished to applaud a toast or speech, they thumped the glass on the table and it made a noise like gunfire.

In the 1740s, what were advertised as 'wormed' or 'wrought' glasses began to appear. The glassmaker, by elongating and twisting a lump of glass containing air bubbles and forming it into a stem, created corkscrew and criss-cross patterns. Today we call these air-twist stem glasses. From 1750 onwards an even more startling result was produced by making similar criss-cross patterns with opaque white or coloured glass threads in the stem. The idea was by no means new, for it was related to the Roman *latticinio* style which the Venetians revived in the sixteenth century, but it was shown off to a peculiar advantage in the long, straight stems of the English glasses.

The last group of drinking glasses which can be categorised by the style of the stem alone is the group of faceted stem glasses. These were cut, usually with diamond- or hexagonal-shaped facets, which covered the stem, the foot, and often the base of the bowl. Most of them have round funnel, ovoid or ogee bowls, and many have a simple engraved pattern on the bowl.

Glasses might be decorated in one of three ways in the eighteenth century; by engraving, enamelling or cutting. Wheel-engraving first became popular in the 1740s with the appearance of the 'flowered' glasses. Scrollwork, flowers, vine-leaves and grapes were the usual motifs of a decorative border on a light baluster glass. But the English wheel-engraving was not of the highest standard, and consequently, English glasses, especially Newcastle glasses, were sent abroad. Much of the work was done in the Netherlands. Many glasses were sent back to England when they had been engraved, but there were other English glasses made in styles not common at home and probably designed specially for foreign markets.

Diamond-point engraving was also popular. It was used, for example, to record political events or to enable the wine-drinker to show his political allegiance—and perhaps tacitly to demand a similar allegiance from his guests. The most sought-after of these are the small group of Jacobite glasses known as 'Amen' glasses from the fact that they had some verses of the Jacobite hymn engraved on them ending with the word Amen. This is probably the only group of English glasses which has been extensively forged. They were made for a small number of important Jacobites, probably personal friends of James, the Old Pretender. It is his cipher— IR8, i.e. Jacobus [Rex VIII—that appears on the glasses. Most of them belonged to Scottish families, and were engraved for them between about 1747 and 1750.

There was a wide variety of less exclusive Jacobite glasses. Most of them, like the 'Amen' glasses, appeared after the Battle of Culloden Moor in 1745, probably over a period of about 20 years. This is curious when one considers the hopelessness of the Jacobite cause after the defeat of 1745. The glasses are engraved with symbols, the most common being the Rose, representing the throne of England, and Rosebuds for the Old Pretender and the Young Pretender. The Thistle is the symbol of the Scottish throne; the Star represents Jacobite endeavour; and the Stricken Oak, the unlucky House of Stuart. There are other symbols whose meanings are less clear. Some glasses also bore Jacobite slogans on the bowl or foot: 'Fiat'; 'Redeat'; 'Health to all our fast friends', etc.

The Williamite glasses were also made in the mid-eighteenth century, probably on the fiftieth anniversary of the Battle of the Boyne, 1690, at which William III defeated James II. Generally, they bear an equestrian portrait, some references to the Boyne, and a quotation from the Orange Lodges' toast. On some of them the Irish harp appears. During the Seven Years War (1756–63) glasses were engraved with ships and portraits of Frederick the Great or Britannia and patriotic mottos. But it was not only the great events that were recorded on glass; many, for example, commemorate fierce local election campaigns.

The finest enamelling on glass is associated with William and Mary Beilby, who worked in Newcastle from about 1762 to 1778. Their helpers included the well-known engraver, Thomas Bewick. They used, generally, a single colour; a bluish- or pinkish-white monochrome. With this they painted fine, delicate designs incorporating peacocks, ruins and obelisks, vines, rural scenes, flowers and fruit. William also did some armorial glasses.

Enamellers also worked on 'Bristol' glass. The name is used for an opaque white glass which has an appearance similar to porcelain. It was made in Bristol, but was certainly made elsewhere, too. The Newcastle glassmakers made Bristol glass, and it may well have been produced in the Midlands. The

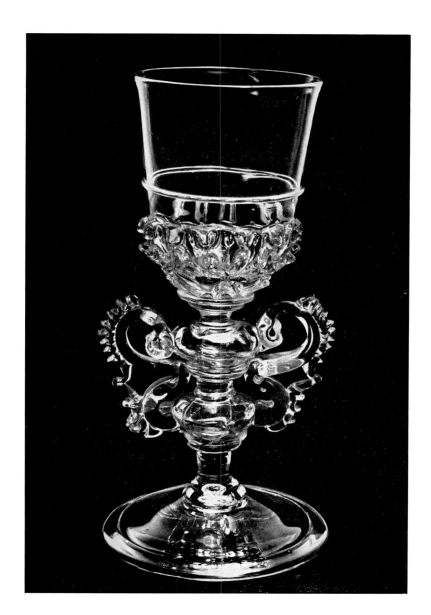

Above: *a funnel bowl goblet engraved with fleur-de-lis and dated 1705.*
Left: *a unique lead glass goblet with extravagant scroll wings on the stem; dated about 1710.*
Below: *a fine 'tazza' of the Ravenscroft period in lead glass on a hollow-pedestal folded foot. Dated about 1675.*

R. D. Pilkington and Sydney Crompton.

71

cream jugs, candlesticks, vases and tea caddies made of 'Bristol' were often painted in oils or varnish and fired, and some were transfer printed. The standard of decoration varies considerably, for some pieces were bought from the factories and decorated by amateur home-craftsmen who sold them to the shops; while others were decorated by professional artists. One such is Michael Edkins, who worked for a number of Bristol glassmakers. Bunches of flowers, scrollwork, birds and *chinoiserie* were the favourite subjects.

Many people consider Bristol Blue to be one of the supreme achievements of the English glassmaker. As with 'Bristol' glass, the name is generic, not geographical. The glassmakers had to go to Bristol to obtain the colouring constituent, 'smalt', which came to the Port of Bristol from Saxony, and so they called it Bristol Blue. The rich colour of this glass is shown off to its best advantage in the wineglasses and the decanters. Many of the latter had the names of drinks gilded on them; and sometimes a gilt label and chain round the neck of the bottle was simulated by means of gilding. Similar objects were also made in other colours, notably bright green.

Nailsea glass, on the other hand, was at first produced exclusively at Nailsea, near Bristol, though the style was later copied in other parts of the country. J. R. Lucas, who was a bottle-maker in Nailsea, decided to take advantage of the lower rate of tax imposed on bottle-glass by making domestic vessels out of it. Two kinds of decoration were developed: the *latticinio* or ribbon effect, which had already been revived for use in the enamel-twist glasses; and the colour-flecking used mainly on the dark Nailsea bottle-glass. The variety of the products of the industry are too numerous to list here, but the *latticinio* flasks are often seen, as are the rolling-pins, tobacco pipes and bells.

Cut glass has had a long and chequered career. Cutting was certainly used on some balustroid glasses. But in 1745/6 an excise duty was imposed on glass based on the weight of the materials, and manufacturers began to reduce the lead content of their glasses and use thinner metal which was not suited to the art of the cutter. Yet cut glass remained popular, though only on the stems of wineglasses could facet cutting still be used, for the bowls would only bear shallow fluting or stars. Then, from 1771 onwards, the excise duty was progressively increased. Ireland, on the other hand, had no such duty until 1825; and there was free trade between the two countries from 1870 onwards. It is no surprise, therefore, to find that many English glassmakers moved to Ireland, and established factories at Waterford and elsewhere. Here they could give full play to their taste for deeply cut glass and massive classical shapes, and as the nineteenth century progressed the style became more and more ponderous. Cut glass returned to English factories when the excise was removed in 1845 in time to perfect, for the Great Exhibition, some of the ugliest glass that has ever been produced. But by then the American technique of press-moulding had made it possible to reproduce cut-glass styles on a mould, and cut glass itself went out of fashion for a while.

There is no space here to deal with the multitude of ephemeral styles in glass that pleased the early Victorians. Few of them produced anything new. The fashion for coloured glass in the 1840s began in Bohemia in the 1820s. Apsley Pellatt's crystallo-ceramic process—by which cameo portraits were enclosed in cut glass objects or paperweights—was borrowed from the French. The English *millefiori* paperweights were barely distinguishable from those the French had been producing before us. This is not to say that all Victorian glass is worthless. The Northwood family, for example, perfected a cameo glass technique which enabled them to make passable imitations of even the Portland Vase. They also perfected the technique of etching on glass, so that the most fragile glasses could be decorated with etched patterns. John Northwood developed the 'intaglio' technique, producing a deeply engraved pattern with the kind of wheel usually used by the glass cutter. Engravers, too, had plenty of opportunity to show off their art on the globular decanters and heavy rummers of the period, and there was so much work that others came from abroad. In the 1880s, two of these, William Fritsche and F. E. Kny were using a 'rock crystal' method of engraving by which the surface of a vase or decanter would be completely covered in a deeply engraved pattern that gave the appearance of carving. But Morris, in 1859, began the revival of good hand-made glass. Thanks to the work of such designers as Philip Webb and Christopher Dresser, and glassmakers such as those at Powell's Whitefriars Glassworks, quality glassmen began to concern themselves more with the design of their glasses than with their decoration, and this is the trend that has continued into the twentieth century.

An English glass engraved with the arms of the United Netherlands. It has a six-sided stem and domed foot. About 1720.

Above: a sweetmeat glass with an eight-sided stem. It has a shallow bowl with applied loops and prunts. About 1750.

Left: three candlesticks with eight-sided pedestal stems. Dated 1740 to 1750.

Right: *two Newcastle glasses. The left is a wineglass with waisted bowl and right a toasting glass with trumpet bowl. Both are dated about 1750.*

Bottom right: *reading left to right, goblet about 1740; wineglass with waisted bowl, about 1730; wineglass with waisted bowl, about 1740; goblet or champagne glass with cup-bowl, about 1750.*
Below: *ale glass with bell bowl, about 1730.*

Left: *wineglass with a drawn trumpet bowl. Inscribed Rich : Spurgeon 1746. Below: a low champagne glass. About 1740.*

Left: *a wineglass with an ogee bowl, and spiral cable air-twist. About 1750.*
Centre: *cordial glass with drawn trumpet bowl. The stem has a vertical gauze with four spiral threads. About 1750.*
Right: *wineglass with round funnel bowl. About 1750.*

A. C. Burton.

Ale glass with bowl engraved with stars and circles. Stem diamond-faceted. About 1770.
R. Dennis.

An 'Amen' glass. The bowl is engraved with two verses of the Jacobite anthem. The stem has a multiple spiral air-twist with beaded knop at the base. About 1750.
A. C. Burton.

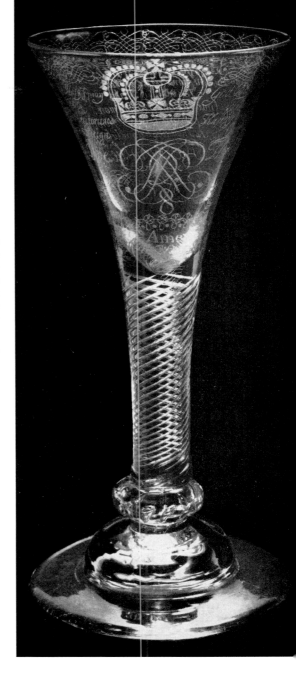

Left: a wineglass with a trumpet bowl, the stem containing a single vertical blue thread and an opaque white multi-ply corkscrew, edged blue. About 1765.
Right: ale glass with round funnel bowl, the stem containing a blue gauze and a pair of white multi-ply spiral bands. About 1765.

Left: *an amethyst colour decanter with spire stopper About 1840.*
Right: *long-necked decanter in clear glass flashed with green and a spire stopper. About 1850.*

Left: *barrel-shaped decanter with mushroom stopper. About 1820.*
Centre: *a variation of design on left. About 1820.*
Right: *decanter with fluted target stopper. About 1820.*

A. C. Burton.

Group of seven Bristol wineglasses in colours varying from peacock blue to dark green. This factory reached a high standard by the start of the nineteenth century.
A. O. Coxon.

Left: *three Bristol Blue condiment bottles with pear stoppers.*
Centre: *a set of Bristol Blue decanters with pear stoppers.*
Right: *Bristol Blue condiment bottle. The labels are in gilt.*
A. O. Coxon.

Left: *jug with serrated rim and horizontal flutes. Lower part with fine diamonds. About 1820.* **Right:** *pitcher-shaped jug with body cut with fine diamond pattern. Made about 1800.*

A. C. Burton

Salad bowl with turned-over cut rim and vertical flutes. Design probably derived from mid-eighteenth century silver bowl. Irish about 1775.

Left: *flask in clear soda-glass splashed red and a little blue. About 1820.*
Right: *bottle in clear lead-glass splashed with red and blue. About 1820.*

Large rummer or goblet on a square base. The bowl is wheel engraved. About 1800.

Left: *rummer with bucket bowl engraved Queen Caroline. About 1820.*
Right: *a bucket bowl rummer engraved with an equestrian portrait of the King's Champion. Bears date July 19 1821.*

Wine flagon and stopper. Possibly from a Stourbridge factory. About 1860.

Goblet in white opaline glass with transfer-print design. Made at Stourbridge mid-nineteenth century.

A mid-nineteenth century paper weight with floral design.
Marjorie Parr.

A small cameo vase with dark red background. Made in late nineteenth century.

Late nineteenth century goblet with engraved bowl on a six-sided stem.

One of a pair of late seventeenth-century pistols by W. Hawkes of Oxford. It was a breech-loaded gun so no ramrod is attached.

Fairclough (Arms) Ltd.

A military blunderbuss pistol dated 1760 which bears the Royal Cipher and the name GALTON. It has a brass barrel.

G. Kellam

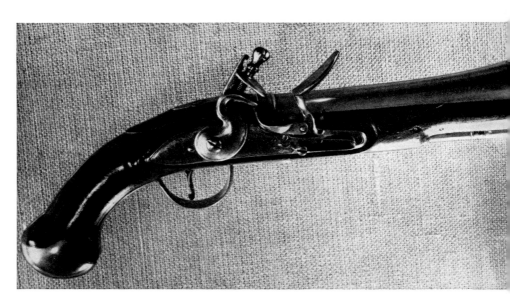

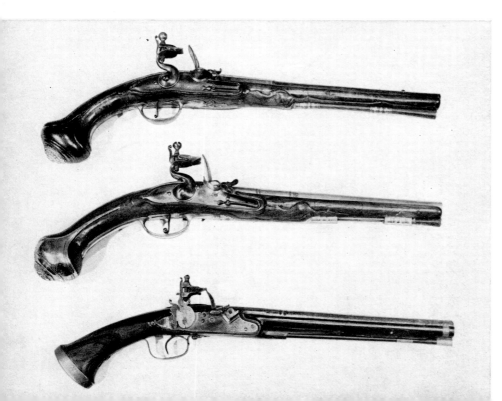

Top: *a flintlock pistol by Barbar, London. About the middle of the seventeenth century.*
Middle: *one of a pair of flintlock pistols by I. Wilson, Dublin.*
Bottom: *an early (c. 1650) English pistol by Ralph Venn.*

R. Chapman.

SMALL ARMS

The Chinese and the Muslims have been credited with the invention of gunpowder, but research tends to dismiss these claims. The best evidence suggests that the Chinese were the first to discover the incendiary qualities of a mixture of charcoal, sulphur and saltpetre some time during the eleventh century. There is no reason to suppose that the Chinese used cannons any earlier than Europeans. How and when the knowledge of gunpowder reached Europe is not clear. There can be no doubt, however, that Roger Bacon knew of its composition in the thirteenth century.

The invention of the cannon is likewise shrouded in mystery, but nearly all the legends ascribe the dubious honour to a German monk of the fourteenth century. The earliest reliable evidence of cannon is usually accepted as being a picture shown in an illustrated manuscript of 1326. A small picture shows a knight about to fire a large vase-shaped container, from the neck of which projects the head of an arrow. It is of interest to note that arrows intended for muskets were still held in the Tower of London stores as late as 1600. Artillery powered by gunpowder was almost certainly used in the Battle of Crécy in 1346, but its effect was more frightening than fatal. The early cannons were usually cast in bronze or copper and were simply barrels fastened to some form of heavy baseboard. They were made in two sections—one a long tube and the other a short cylinder closed at one end. Into this small chamber went the powder and a projectile of stone or iron. The chamber was then locked into position against the end of the barrel. The tip of a red hot iron was placed into a small touch hole situated at the top of the chamber and the cannon fired. The gunner often stood in as much peril as his enemy, for it was not uncommon for the weapon to explode killing all the crew.

In general, artillery was used only in siege warfare, blasting holes in city or castle walls and demolishing defences, and the guns were usually fixed and not easily transportable. However, it was not long before the idea of a small, easily portable weapon was developed and the so-called handgun was the result. These simple tubes of iron varied in length from a few inches to several feet but were almost invariably mounted on long wooden stocks. The body was cast in one piece and the powder and ball were inserted by way of the muzzle. Some of the early cannons were loaded in the same way. Aiming was almost impossible; at best the weapon was unreliable and at worst completely useless.

In a document of 1418 there occurs the first mention of a hackbut or hookgun which was the first firearm that could be said to be aimed. The long tube was fitted to a wooden stock from which projected a hook or lug to fit over a wall and by so doing reduced the kick-back or recoil. These early handguns were noisy, unreliable and often ineffective but, nevertheless, they represented the beginning of a revolution in warfare. The longbow required a great deal of skill in its use and long training was necessary; the crossbow was slow and expensive to make; but the handgun was a weapon that could be produced cheaply and in quantity. An absolute minimum of skill was required and only the thickest, and hence the most cumbersome, of armour was protection against the bullet. It was the beginning of the end for armour although it was not to disappear for several centuries.

Examples of these early handguns are extremely rare. In appearance they are very similar to the original type; but, in fact, there is every reason to believe that they are of comparatively recent manufacture originating in the East.

The necessity of some means of heating the 'firing' wire severely limited the mobility of the hand gunner, but by the middle of the fifteenth century this restriction had been removed by the introduction of the slowmatch. A length of cord was boiled in a solution containing, among other things, saltpetre, and then allowed to dry. When the cord was lit it burned slowly with a glowing end which could be used to fire the charge of powder. The operation was entirely manual at first but the addition of an S-shaped lever, or serpentine, rendered it automatic. This lever was fixed to the side of the stock, the glowing end of the match was fastened at the top of the serpentine and pressure on the lower section depressed the glowing end on to the touch hole. The matchlock, as this new weapon was called, was at first nothing more than the old handgun equipped with a serpentine, but soon the stock was adapted and by the early sixteenth century it had a pronounced downward curve. By about 1530 the matchlock had taken on its most characteristic form, and from Italy this style spread northwards, reaching England via the Low Countries.

The arquebus was long-barrelled, heavy and cumbersome. The stock was usually quite plain although some specimens were inlaid with mother-of-pearl, ivory and bone. The high combed butt was cut away to facilitate a good grip. The barrel, up to forty inches long and weighing anything up to twenty pounds, was so heavy that it was impossible to hold the weapon steady enough to aim. The musketeer overcame this problem by means of an ash staff surmounted by a U-shaped holder. With this rest he could prop up the barrel and so take aim.

The simple, hand-operated serpentine was replaced by a system of levers operated by a long bar or trigger. During the early part of the sixteenth century a snaplock had been in use, but was discarded as being unsafe: the arm which held the glowing slowmatch was at rest with the match pressed into the pan. To prepare for firing the arm was pulled up, away from the pan, and held in that position by means of a small projection. When a stud or trigger was pressed the arm was released and, impelled by a spring, moved forward and down to ignite the priming. The danger of accidental discharge is obvious and for this reason the more usual matchlock mechanism became common. Here the arm at rest was away from the pan; pressure on the lever or trigger swung the arm forward and down to fire the weapon; immediately pressure was removed the arm rose up and away from the pan. A great many of these muskets were fitted with a small tube above the breech and this served as a peep sight. A smaller, lighter version of the arquebus was known as a 'caliver'.

It is very unlikely that the average collector will acquire a European matchlock, but it is still easy to find a similar weapon made in the Orient. The Portuguese sailors reached India at the end of the fifteenth century and, of course, their matchlocks went with them. The Indians were greatly impressed by these marvellous weapons and sought to acquire them for their own use. Soon the Indian swordsmiths and armourers were applying their very considerable skills to the production of gunbarrels. Unlike most European barrels these were commonly inlaid with gold or embellished in some other way. The stocks were made from many beautiful woods and again were richly decorated with any number of materials. The matchlock was made in India right up until the beginning of the present century and many of the Indian princes had armouries filled with fine quality weapons.

The Portuguese were also responsible for the introduction of the matchlock to Japan, and the Japanese began to manufacture them as well. Japan is a rather special case, and owing to the country's isolation Japanese gunmaking jumped from matchlock to cartridge weapons with little or none of the intermediate developments which took place in Europe. Japanese matchlocks are easily recognised with their rather thick barrels, short stocks and generally stubby butts. The barrels are usually of very fine quality whereas their springs tend to be rather weak and ineffective. The snaplock, long discarded in Europe, is usually found on Japanese weapons. Japanese swordsmiths were experts in metal work and their skill produced some exquisitely decorated barrels. Brass and silver inlay were common and brass decoration is often found on the stock as well. Japan also produced matchlock pistols ranging from a normal size down to tiny specimens only a few inches long, and it is difficult to believe that these tiny ones were anything more than toys or models.

There is one common feature of nearly all Eastern matchlocks, and that is in the operation of the serpentine. It is true to say that, with few exceptions, all European matchlocks have the serpentine moving towards the butt, but almost invariably the Eastern matchlock has the serpentine moving the opposite way, i.e. towards the barrel. There seems to be little to recommend one system or the other and it is rather difficult to see how the two systems remained so different. It may be that Eastern conservatism, or love of tradition, preserved the original mechanism of the first European matchlocks that went to the East, although it seems rather unlikely that this is the real reason.

In Europe the matchlock continued in use until the end of the seventeenth century. The gunmakers had, however, sought some simpler system of producing a flame or spark to ignite the priming of the gun. The first practical solution was the wheellock. The lock, which first appears at the beginning of the sixteenth century, was self-igniting and, unlike the match, was ready for use at a moment's notice. The principle was simple— nothing more than rubbing a piece of mineral known as pyrites against a rough-edged,

A blunderbuss or 'musketoon' dating from about 1750. It has a brass barrel.
G. Kellam.

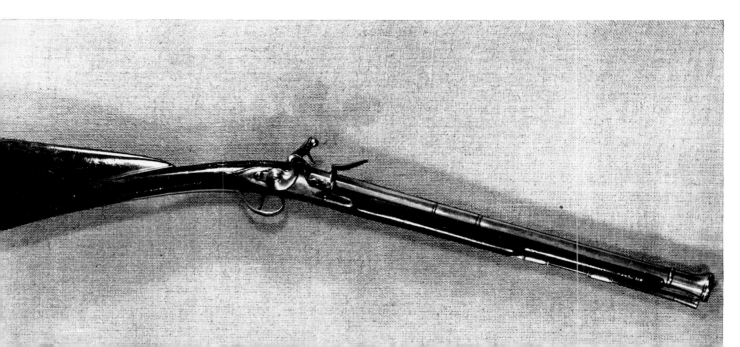

steel wheel. The operating mechanism was rather complicated, consisting of a strong, V-shaped spring which was compressed by rotating a key or spanner. When fully wound the wheel was held by a sear or locking bar; pressure on the trigger withdrew the locking bar and allowed the spring, via a short linked chain, to rotate the wheel very rapidly. The grooved edge of the wheel struck sparks from the pyrites and ignited the priming and hence the main charge of powder. The pyrites was held between the jaws of an angled arm known as the doghead.

The early wheellocks were fitted with various safety devices and gadgets, and a good working generalisation is that the simpler the lock plate, i.e. the fewer the knobs and buttons, the later the weapon.

The wheellock was fitted to all types of weapons and many matchlocks were altered to take this new system. The expense precluded entire armies being equipped with wheellocks, but many select groups such as bodyguards and special cavalry troops were armed with them. The nobility ordered fine hunting weapons fitted with this new lock as well as pistols for their own use. Great skill was lavished on the weapons, and many are works of art in their own right. Stocks and barrels were engraved, inlaid, chiselled—decorated in every conceivable style and material.

Most wheellock hunting weapons have a curious barrel-heavy appearance; this is because a very heavy barrel was fitted to reduce the recoil, and the butt was much shorter than the more usual shoulder stock since the weapon was fired, not from the shoulder, but with the butt resting against the cheek. Despite its advantages it was not without its faults. Its very complexity was a great weakness, for mechanical failure was not uncommon, and only a fairly skilled man could hope to repair any such faults. It was also expensive to produce. Some writers of the period also claimed that it was liable to jamming.

However, once the idea of mechanically produced sparks proved practical it was not long before a simpler, more reliable method was discovered. This was the snaphaunce, or snaphance, lock which appeared in the mid-sixteenth century. The pyrites of the wheellock was replaced by the commoner flint, and in place of the wheel and chain a simpler mechanical system was used. The piece of flint was held firmly between two jaws at the top of a curved arm or cock; the pan was covered, as in the wheellock, by a sliding cover, and just above the pan cover was a steel plate at the end of a metal arm. Loading and priming were essentially the same as for the wheellock. After their execution the steel was lowered into position above the closed pan cover; the cock was pulled back, compressing the spring, and held in this position. On pressing the trigger the cock was released and flew forward allowing the flint to strike the steel which was then pushed back out of the way; the sparks thus fell into the pan which had been uncovered by the automatic removal of the pan cover; the priming flashed and, via the touch-hole, fired the main charge. The snaphaunce was used for only a comparatively short period in Europe and these weapons are very rare indeed, but, like the matchlock, the system was retained elsewhere long after it had been discarded in Europe.

The snaphaunce was simply a stepping stone to the next system, the flintlock. The essential difference between the two systems is that the flintlock has the pancover and steel united into one L-shaped piece known by a variety of names such as steel, hammer or frizzen. This combination of the two pieces simplified the internal mechanism, and the flintlock was to remain in use for some 250 years, reaching an extremely high standard of efficiency and reliability.

The true flintlock probably originated in France early in the seventeenth century. Although it was in use for such a long period it is still possible to date a flintlock weapon with reasonable ease, for there were fashions in guns as there were fashions in clothes. The earlier locks are rather banana-shaped with a slightly concave surface, while later locks tend to be flat and straighter. Some care is necessary here, for many of the seventeenth-century locks also had flat lock-plates. Triggers also changed, and earlier ones tend to be much straighter and simpler. The butt is a useful guide in dating, for many of the earlier seventeenth-century pistols tend to terminate with a flat, cut-off appearance; late seventeenth-century and early eighteenth-century pistols are usually found with a large swelling, or pommel, which tends to decrease in size as the century progresses, until it disappears altogether at the end of the eighteenth century. Late eighteenth-century and early nineteenth-century butts tend to be rather like hockey sticks in shape. Again, most of the pommels were fitted with a metal covering known as a butt cap. These butt caps were sometimes plain but after the early years of the eighteenth century they were decorated with grotesque heads. In the early eighteenth-century flintlocks the spurs of the butt cap extended well up the butt, and as the century progressed these tended to shorten and finally disappear except for a slight curve on the side of the cap.

The flintlock was basically simple to construct and, in consequence, was produced in quantity. It spread from Europe to Africa, America and Asia. Like the wheellock it could be made in any size and consequently will be found ranging from massive locks for wall pieces and cannon through pocket pistols to tiny miniature locks only a fraction of an inch long.

The simplicity of the flintlock meant that manufacturing costs were low, and it could be supplied in bulk at reasonable prices. In Britain the matchlock was completely abandoned by the end of the seventeenth century, and the musket known to all collectors as the 'Brown Bess' was introduced about 1720. This simple, sturdy yet elegant weapon was to remain the principal arm of the British infantry right up until the middle of the nineteenth century. Design and detail varied over the years, but it remained essentially the same weapon. There were three main types with barrels of 46 inches, 42 inches and 39 inches. The first two were the earliest and are now also the rarest; the 39-inch, usually referred to as the India Pattern, was produced in great numbers during the Napoleonic Wars and is, therefore, much more common. A bayonet could be attached to the end of the barrel of all three by means of a simple socket device.

Sporting guns were made with flintlocks and many are double-barrelled, fitted with a lock on each barrel and operated by separate triggers. A tremendous amount of effort went into the manufacture of highest-quality gun barrels, and a considerable mystique developed. Long and earnest discussions were held by sportsmen on the best type of barrel, shot and powder, and many gunmakers became renowned for their high-quality work in this field.

In the seventeenth century and early eighteenth century the majority of pistols were large and made primarily for horsemen, but the growth of coach travel and the increase of crime in towns created a demand for smaller, more personal pistols. These so-called travelling pistols were intended to fit into the pockets of great coats or into travelling bags. For self protection the pocket and muff pistols were produced. These ranged from some four to six inches in length. Many were double-barrelled, and others, after the end of the eighteenth century, were fitted with a bayonet which was folded back along the barrels; when required it could be released to fly forward and lock into position.

Much more popular for defence of the home was the blunderbuss. This short weapon had a barrel with a bore which increased in diameter towards the muzzle. The wide mouth probably produced a louder than normal explosion, thus increasing the overall effect of the weapon. The blunderbuss was popular in the seventeenth century and continued so until the mid-nineteenth century when the revolver tended to displace it as the chief personal weapon. Contrary to popular belief it did not fire rusty nails, broken glass or rubbish, the normal load being a number of small lead balls.

Just as some makers acquired a reputation for sporting guns, others acquired similar reputations for duelling weapons. Wogden was probably the best known in the late eighteenth century. In true duelling pistols the barrels are usually heavy, frequently octagonal, and the butt is very gently curved to fit the hand when in the aiming position. Some are equipped with an extension to the trigger guard and this so-called spur ensured a firmer grip. Since the normal pressure required to squeeze the trigger was quite substantial there was a danger of going off target while squeezing. The hair, or set, trigger was a series of levers which could be adjusted so that only the merest touch was required to fire the weapon. Sometimes a single trigger serves as the normal and the hair trigger, but in other weapons a second trigger is fitted. Many of the so-called duelling pistols around today are, however, ordinary target pistols.

Many of the famous makers such as Nock, Manton and Egg improved the design and construction of the flintlock, and by the 1820s it was probably at its most efficient. However, there were certain inherent difficulties which could not be overcome by any improvement; the flint itself was only reliable for a certain number of shots—thirty was usually reckoned as a safe maximum—and the chances of a misfire were high. Even more serious was the 'hangfire'; this was the small, but nevertheless appreciable, timelag between the pressing of the trigger and the explosion, and the delay was obviously a great disadvantage when aiming at a moving target.

The Reverend Alexander Forsyth of Belhelvie in Aberdeenshire, was the first to hit upon a practical solution to these problems. He had a fair working knowledge of chemistry and knew that certain chemicals or fulminates would explode on impact. Since the explosion produced a flame he reasoned that this flash could be used to ignite the charge in firearms. By 1805 he had made a

lock which produced a spark by the exploding of a chemical. This so-called percussion lock was not the complete answer, but at least the idea was shown to be sound and feasible. Forsyth came to London and worked on his idea, part of the time in the Tower of London. He used loose fulminating powder, and other designers attempted to overcome the obvious hazards of this system by packing the powder in pills and tubes. The system that proved most satisfactory, however, was that using a little copper cap; the cap, shaped rather like a top hat, had a small quantity of fulminate deposited on the inside and the cap fitted snugly over a pillar drilled with a tiny hole which communicated with the main charge. The credit for the invention of this simple, but highly effective, device was claimed by many, but it is now generally thought that Joshua Shaw, an Englishman living in America, has the greatest claim.

The percussion cap was much less prone to misfire, its hangfire was considerably reduced, and it was also quicker and simpler to use than the flintlock. Many owners of fine pistols or guns sought to prolong the life of their flintlock by converting it to the new system. Several types of conversion were used, but probably the most common was the pillar system whereby a peg or nipple was set into a small tube which fitted over the touch-hole. Steel, pan cover and frizzen spring were removed and the cock replaced by a hammer. Converted weapons are fairly common but, in general, they are not popular with collectors and usually fetch a lower price than a similar piece with its original flintlock.

The introduction of the copper cap opened the way to a flood of new ideas, but the most important was that of repeating weapons. Revolvers had been made using the matchlock, snaphaunce and flintlock but almost without exception they were difficult to construct, inefficient, unpopular and in many cases positively dangerous. Samuel Colt had manufactured a very efficient and practical revolver in the 1830s but, despite its many advantages, it did not achieve any really widespread popularity until the 1850s, when it ousted the old-fashioned pepperbox.

The pepperbox was essentially a series of tubes drilled into a solid cylinder block. Each barrel was loaded and capped; the cylinder was rotated mechanically or by hand as each was fired. The length of the cylinder was subsequently reduced, and the transition revolver came into being. It was in essence a cut-down pepperbox with a single barrel serving each tube.

In England Colt's main rivals were Adams, Tranter and Webley, although numerous other makers produced revolvers. Adams was probably the greatest competitor, and the arguments as to the relative merit of the two weapons waxed long and hard. One of the biggest points of controversy was over the mechanical systems. In Colt revolvers the hammer had to be pulled back by the thumb, and the weapon was then fired by pressing the trigger. Adams and many other gunsmiths favoured the system whereby pressure on the trigger rotated the cylinder, lifted the hammer and eventually fired the weapon.

Colt revolvers were prominently displayed at the Great Exhibition of 1851 held in London. Numerous engraved presentation weapons were distributed to all who Colt felt would be impressed. Eventually he set up a factory in London to manufacture his revolvers. His English competitors made great efforts to reduce his lead in the field, and although he became one of the greatest manufacturers of firearms, exporting all over the world, he closed his London factory in 1856. Colt revolvers never achieved in Britain that tremendous popularity which was theirs in America and many other countries.

By the middle of the nineteenth century Birmingham and London were the great centres of the arms industry, and apart from some provincial craftsmen who managed to stay in business the majority of firearms of this period will have been made in one of these two cities.

When the British army finally accepted the obvious superiority of the percussion system, tests were carried out to find the most suitable adaptation for general issue. The old Brown Bess was converted to percussion and soon the entire British army was equipped with the new arm.

From the 1850s firearm development was swift and impressive. The percussion cap was primarily responsible, for it enabled inventors to produce a tremendous variety of breech-loading and repeating weapons—many of which were extremely impracticable. The use of fulminate also stimulated the designers of ammunition, and soon cartridges, containing their own source of ignition, were appearing; by the 1860s metal-case cartridges, with the priming cap set on the centre of the base, were coming into general use.

The introduction of the centre-fire cartridge was really the last step in the production of modern firearms. Powder was soon abandoned and more efficient and powerful explosives introduced; bullets were improved in design and performance, and highly efficient mechanical repeating-devices were introduced, though these are all merely improvements on the basic weapon of the 1860s and 70s.

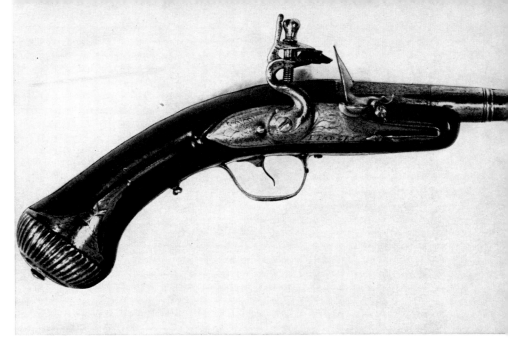

An English flintlock pistol by J. Tarles and made between 1650 and 1660. These pistols were loaded by unscrewing the barrel and placing the powder and shot in the breech.

D. S. H. Gyngell.

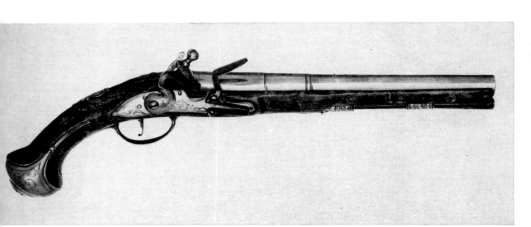

One of a pair of English pistols. It bears the name of I. Hall and was made about 1680.

G. Knowles.

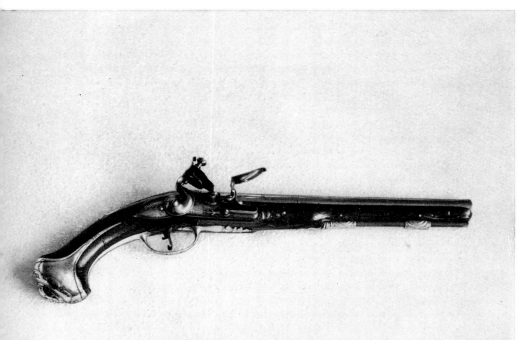

A flintlock holster pistol bears the name I. Reed and was made about 1710. It has a carved stock and silver mounts.

A. Littler.

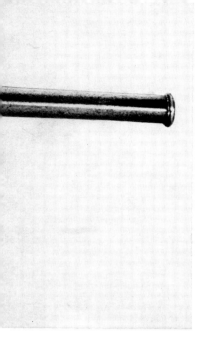

Top: *a small musket or 'fusil' of the late seventeenth century. The lock plate bears the Royal Cipher, 'W.R.', below a crown.*
Bottom: *another musket but of early eighteenth-century date. The lock plate bears the name 'R. Wolldridge'.*

H.M. Tower of London.

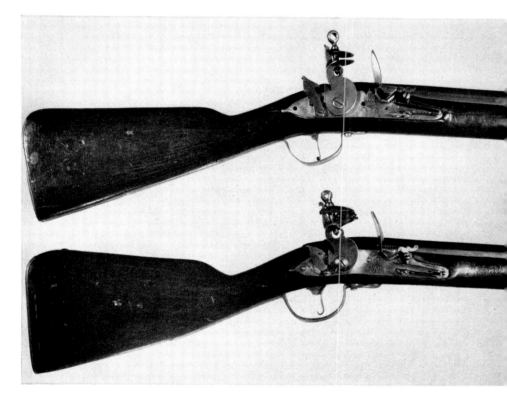

A pocket flintlock pistol by John Harman of London and made about 1690. It is fitted with a ball-trigger which is unusual on the weapons, as is the fore-end which unscrews from the barrel.

H. L. Blackmore.

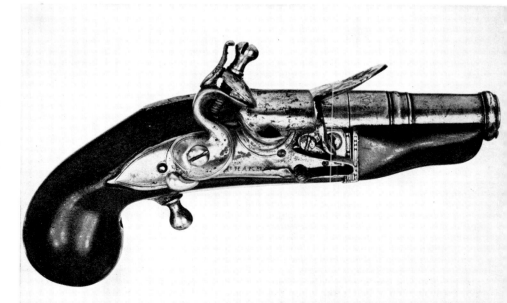

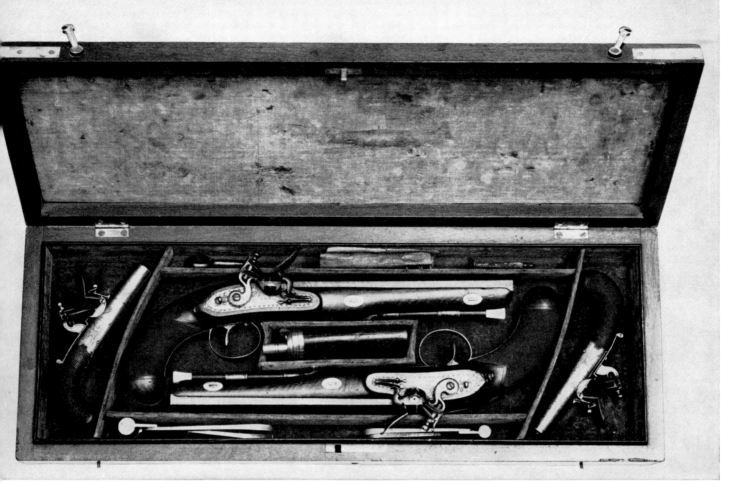

A cased set containing two pocket pistols marked 'Stokes and Co.' and two holster pistols marked 'Stokes and Hunt'. Each pistol has the initials 'T.A.' on the silver escutcheon.
Fairclough (Arms) Ltd.

A pocket pistol by H. Nock, made about 1800.
The slab-sided butt is inlaid with a design in silver wire.
D. S. H. Gyngell.

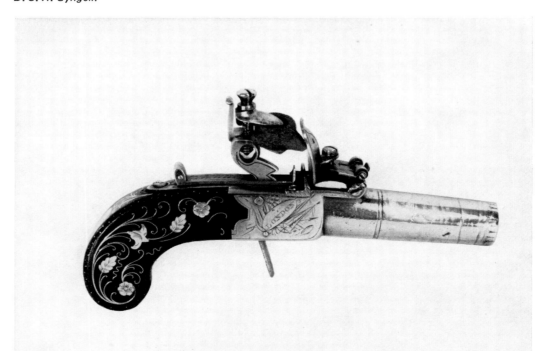

94

A pistol with a detachable stock. These were introduced with the idea of converting them into carbines. The stock and the barrel were made by Durs Egg.

G. Kellam.

A pocket pistol with over and under barrels. Its silver butt cap bears the date 1789 and the breech is inscribed 'Meredith' on one side and 'Chester' on the other.

D. S. H. Gyngell.

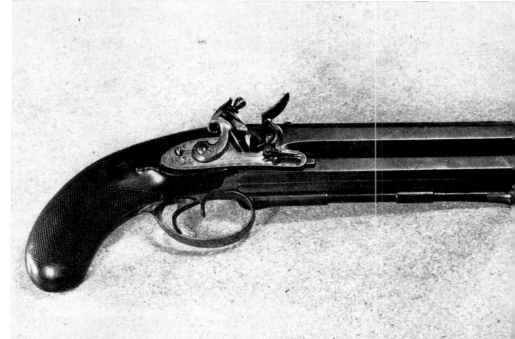

A double-barrelled over and under pistol by Durs Egg, a Swiss born gunmaker and one of the most famous of London gunmakers.

G. E. Bennett.

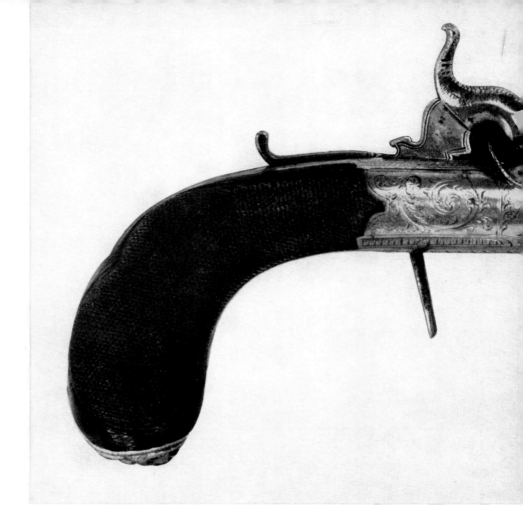

A double-barrelled percussion pistol with swivel ramrod. Made by John Bissett, 321 High Holborn, London.

D. S. H. Gyngell.

One of a pair of percussion pocket pistols. The breech is inscribed 'Marton' and 'London'. The weapon has a concealed trigger.

D. S. H. Gyngell.

An eighteenth-century pistol converted from flint to percussion cap. The weapon is marked T. Jackson, Maidstone.

G. E. Bennett.

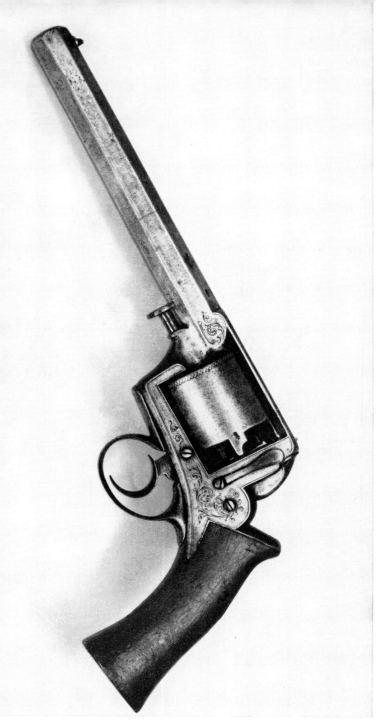

An English revolver patented by Robert Adams in 1851. These revolvers were cocked and fired by pressure on the trigger and did not require cocking manually.
Dominion Museum of New Zealand.

A New Model pocket pistol made by Colt in London. This design was made from 1861–1872. The barrel is engraved with a scene of a stage-coach hold-up !
S. Durrant.

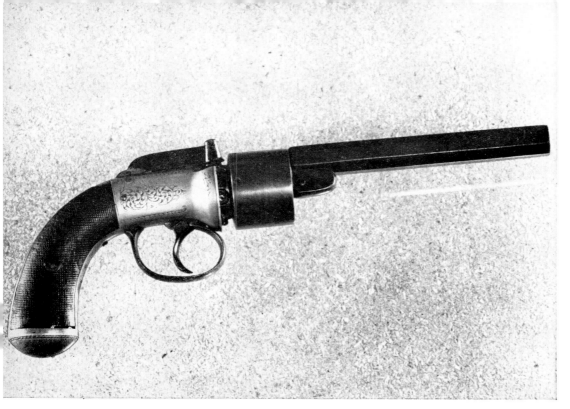

A transition revolver which was produced in quantity especially in Birmingham, in the nineteenth century.
G. E. Bennett.

A Tranter double-triggered revolver. The case is of mahogany lined with green baize.
E. Perry.

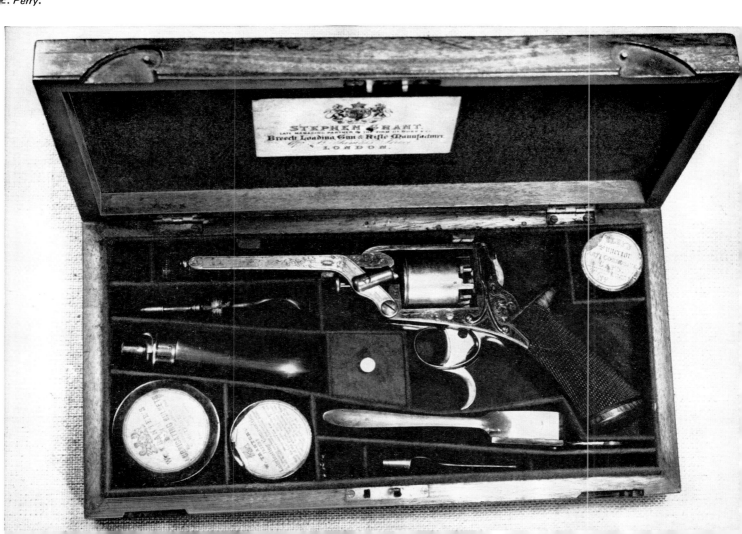

A magnificent bed dated 1585 and made of walnut with fine panels of inlaid box and holly. The wood is not profusely carved as so many were of this period. It has great simplicity and dignity.
H. W. Keil Ltd.

FURNITURE

Of all domestic items, furniture is probably the most interesting to collect—and the most competed for. Throughout its long history it has reflected, year by year, the changes in social conditions, the ebb and flow in this taste and that taste, the constantly changing habits of the people, the contrast between rich and poor, and the power of the community that made and used it to exercise authority over distant parts of the world and extract their riches. Silver, porcelain, jewellery and pewter are all dispensable; during periods of strife—such as the Commonwealth—they were hardly made at all. But even in war, men have a need, though a limited need, for furniture; and consequently furniture provides a continuous record of their needs and tastes.

In its design, furniture is closely related to architecture: the design of the inside of a house is a composition of furniture, carefully made and distributed, so that we find that all manner of architects turned their hands to furniture design. William Kent, Robert Adam and Charles Rennie Mackintosh are outstanding examples. Of course, this is to use the word 'furniture' in a very wide sense, but even if we were to exclude glass, porcelain, silver, chandeliers, fire-irons, carpets and paintings, it would still be true to say that the remaining articles—the tables and chairs and cabinets—are the most significant and imposing items in a room. They, together with the proportions of the room itself, and the shape of the windows, doors and fireplace, make up the design of the room, though they may be marred or enhanced by the lesser contributors to the whole.

For the greater part of the Middle Ages there was very little furniture, either in the manor or in the cottage. What furniture there was was generally portable, for the living space, even in the manor-house, was used for many purposes; it was only in monasteries and some of the greater castles that rooms were divided up according to their function. Tables were usually of the trestle type, made of oak, and had benches drawn up to them, for only the most important members of society were allowed to sit in chairs. The most comfortable thing the ordinary person was likely to sit on was the settle, a bench with a high back and an arm at each end, and usually decorated with linen-fold panelling. The bed was the most valuable piece of furniture in any house, but even this could be dismantled and stored away. Lowly people, such as servants and students, had truckle beds, which were so low that they could be pushed away under a larger bed during the day. Things were stored in aumbrys, or in small chests which could also be used as side-tables. In general, medieval furniture was not prestige stuff, though there were magnificent linen-fold dressers and state beds made. It was sturdily built, and the better pieces would be decorated with Gothic tracery in keeping with their surroundings, but not in any attempt to conceal their real purpose and shape, as in the neo-Gothic furniture of the nineteenth century.

A William II 'seaweed' marquetry side table. It has ebonised borders and turned ebony bosses. Note the double-scroll legs of square section.

Christie, Manson & Woods Ltd.

In the sixteenth century, furniture appeared that reflected the more settled lives that people lived under the Tudors. Houses now began to be divided up so that the whole family, not just the head of the house, could have some privacy. Bedrooms still remained fairly bare of furniture, but the parlours that began to appear at this time might have a number of pieces in them. The overall effect of the Tudor interior was rather dark, for the walls were covered with oak panelling and the furniture was mainly of dark oak, but some colour could be added to the scene by tapestries or embroidered upholstery. The bed became an altogether more permanent and imposing piece of furniture, its four heavy posts bearing a carved wooden canopy, or 'tester', over the top of the bed, which contained decorated panelling. The headposts merged into the panelling at the head of the bed in the mid-sixteenth century and disappeared, while a feature of the remaining two posts, and of the legs of tables in the late sixteenth century, was the decorative bulb, said to have been introduced to England by the Huguenot refugees. These bulbs continued in use in the seventeenth century, and in fact reached their greatest size during the reign of James I, when they quite dominated the appearance of a piece

of furniture. Another feature of the late-sixteenth century is the panel-back chair, which replaced the linen-fold chairs and the X-shape chairs of Henry VIII's day. The day-bed, a narrow bed with an adjustable headpiece for relaxing during the day, was probably brought to England by the foreign craftsmen whom Henry VIII introduced to work on his new palaces. In any case, they became a feature of the late Tudor household, for Shakespeare speaks at one point of 'lolling upon a lewd daybed'. Court cupboards, which appeared in the early sixteenth century, consisted of two tiers of open shelves, and were used to store cups, flagons, silver vessels and the like. Livery cupboards, through which air was allowed to circulate by means of balustered doors or openwork panels, were more suitable for food.

The quality of life continued to improve even more rapidly during the seventeenth century, and, after the Restoration, there began the period of elegance and magnificence that was to last until the social upheavals of the early nineteenth century. Furniture changed as the style of building changed from the Tudor mansions, with their large windows composed of long, thin lights, to the redbrick manor houses of the late-seventeenth century gentry and the Baroque extravagances of Blenheim. The rich discarded their heavy oak beds and replaced them with lighter, beechwood constructions, tall and slender and draped with hangings. At the four corners of the tester there appeared vase-shaped finials, covered with material and topped with ostrich plumes. The bed had ceased to be homely and become a fit subject for display. In the last third of the century, marquetry became popular, and so, for the first time, did the taste for Chinese decoration. Both forms embellished late-seventeenth century cabinets, and they were succeeded by quieter arabesque patterns, and inlaid brass and tortoise-shell. The chest of drawers, which came into its own for the first time after the Restoration when extravagant dress was again acceptable, was similarly treated, at first with polychromatic designs in marquetry of birds and flowers, and later, during William III's reign, with the overall 'seaweed' patterning of monochrome marquetry, drawn from the arabesque lines of the endive plant. Not that all forms of furniture followed the dictates of fashion, both in style and decoration, as interpreted in the Home Counties of England. The cupboard, for example, was a piece that continued to have a local life of its own, even in the eighteenth century. One example is the *cwpwedd tridarn* of Wales, predecessor of the farmhouse dresser.

Chairs became more sophisticated too. Panel-back chairs continued to be made until the 1660s, but after the Restoration there appeared chairs with backs formed of turned balusters, and twisted legs. There was a new accent on comfort, too, with the appearance of the upholstered, winged armchair. The settee was another late-seventeenth century development, derived partly from the settle, partly from an expansion of the chair. In its early days it looked rather like two or more chairs stuck together, for its length was divided up by arms and its back was formed of a series of chair backs, either open or upholstered.

The long dining-table became obsolete in the late seventeenth century, for it was now more acceptable to dine even a large company in groups round small, scattered tables. For this, the gateleg table was more suitable. This, usually rather plain, table was normally round or oval when its flaps were extended. The side-table was a better subject for decoration, for the examples delicately carved by the hand of Grinling Gibbons, master of the art of carving flowers, fruit and birds in a startlingly realistic manner, are by no means normal among the side-tables of the later seventeenth century. The Restoration side-table was of walnut, and had twisted or baluster legs; while the French influence followed in the train of William II, so that side-tables displayed tapered legs with gadrooned capitals, foliated strapwork pendants and elaborately scrolled stretchers.

A Queen Anne faded walnut kneehole desk. It was made about 1710.

Mallett & Son (Antiques) Ltd.

The development of seventeenth century furniture was rather haphazard, in comparison with that of the eighteenth century. All kinds of influences were at work, both from home and from abroad, and furniture makers were affected by the decorative ideas of such men as Grinling Gibbons and Daniel Marot. But in the eighteenth and early nineteenth centuries, though design continued to be affected by ideas from all kinds of quarters—the taste for *chinoiserie* and the Gothic style are examples—yet the work of the designers was far more important. They introduced some consistency into furniture design. By no means was every piece of work made from their designs, yet almost every piece was affected by the publication of such books of design as Chippendale's *Gentleman and Cabinet-Maker's Director*, which made them known to everyone in the furniture trade.

The outstanding designers of this period were William Kent, Thomas Chippendale, Robert Adam, George Hepplewhite and Thomas Sheraton. Kent (1684–1748) was by no means exclusively a furniture designer. He began as a painter, and later became an architect, a sculptor, and even helped to establish the style of the eighteenth century English landscape garden. His studies in

Italy made him an enthusiastic follower of Palladio, and when he began to design furniture in England it was the architectural motifs to which he had become so attached that he developed. As a result his furniture was on the grand scale, and pieces such as his vast, pedimented bookcases, were suited only to the new Palladian mansions that were appearing in the English countryside at this time. Even his settees were formal in design, made rather to suit the room than to accommodate the people who used the room.

The London cabinet-maker Thomas Chippendale (1718–1779) had a much wider-ranging talent as a furniture designer, for he assimilated the new fashions as they appeared, and produced his own finely designed versions of the Rococo style, the Chinese Taste and the Gothic Taste, and, late in his career, the Neo-classical style. His beds were lighter in appearance than those of his predecessors, with carved mahogany posts, cabriole legs on lion's feet and delicately carved shafts. His bookcases too, though they included architectural motifs such as the broken pediment, were altogether lighter than Kent's pieces. Many remember him best for the design of his chairs, like the ribbon-back, and the classical chairs with oval, heart or shield-shaped backs, and the tapered classical leg in place of the cabriole leg.

What Robert Adam (1728–1792) sought to do in furniture differs not at all from his work as an architect, for he conceived architecture and furniture as merely different facets of the same problem of design. The motifs of the neo-classical style that he developed from his observations of the Palace of Diocletian at Spalato are too well known to need to be described here. Adam admired 'the rise and fall, the advance and recess, and other diversity of forms' in a building, as well as 'a variety of light mouldings', and it was the same principles that he applied in his interiors, such as that magnificent example, the library at Syon House. Here the pastel shade walls are decorated with classical style mouldings in white, and the circular portraits in oils do not exist in their own right but all form part of the overall design.

George Hepplewhite, who died in 1786, was another London furniture maker whose designs were published after his death as *The Cabinet-maker and Upholsterer's Guide*. The Neo-classical style was a strong influence in his work. There are Hepplewhite bookcases, for example, with straight moulded cornices, surmounted by an urn or some scrollwork, and the doors banded with satinwood and sometimes enriched with an inlay of figures. His beds had slender posts carved with wheatears, and cornices inlaid or painted with flowers or ribbons; and his chairs had the classical motifs of shield- or heart-shaped backs.

Thomas Sheraton (1750–1806) straddles both the late eighteenth century period and the Regency. He published a number of books of design, notably the *Cabinet-maker and Upholsterer's Drawing Book* and the *Cabinet-maker's Dictionary*. His early style had a great deal in common with the work of Hepplewhite, but his bookcases, for example, tended to be narrower with rather stilted proportions, and to include features such as swan-necks and serpentine pediments, unusual finials, and satinwood veneers. He used the classical urn as a feature in some of his chairs in the 1790s, as well as making square-back chairs.

The Regency style, probably the strangest style in the whole history of English furniture, was pioneered by the architect Sir John Soane, and Thomas Hope, a writer and amateur furniture designer. The style was based, in part at least, on a close study of Roman interior decoration, though the Egyptian sphinx was also imported. The whole effect must have been extremely severe. There were sofas that followed the supposed design of Roman couches, with a low back curved over at one end, and the tripod table that the Romans had made in marble was reproduced in wood. Lion masks and swans were frequent features of the style, as was the remarkably ugly hocked animal leg support, topped by a cat or lion head. Many of the decorative features were made of brass, so

that there was no need for the furniture makers to have any skill in carving. Alternatively, items such as chairs might be made of beechwood painted black, and decorated with a design in gold.

It was obvious that a profound change was bound to come over furniture as the nineteenth century progressed. The furniture makers no longer had to deal with a small class of rich men who had both the leisure and the inclination to concern themselves with matters of taste. England had a growing Middle Class, all of whom wanted to dress up their houses as they thought was befitting to their station, and so the manufacturers, flooded with orders, sought to do the job more rapidly and brought in machinery. But new techniques do not at once bring new styles, and it was not really until the twentieth century that people began to realise that machinery could produce fine furniture, but only if that furniture was designed with the capabilities of the machine process in mind.

The Victorians used machinery to make their furniture, but they tried at the same time to make the same kind of furniture as their forefathers had made—with certain improvements. Two things were required of a piece of furniture: that it should be comfortable, if it was going to be sat on, and

that it should be imposing. The result: massive armchairs, that look even heavier than they really are, profusely decorated with carving, and every piece of the structure curving and bulging this way and that; or massive pieces of 'Gothic' furniture, whether they be like Pugin's cabinets, covered all over with Gothic designs, or the plainer, sturdy and austere beds, washbasins and cabinets designed by William Burges. The first sign of change came in the 1870s with Morris and the Arts and Crafts Movement. Part of this was backward-looking, with its accent on hand-produced furniture of a medieval simplicity. But, on the other hand, it created a new interest in design, in creating furniture that was suited to its function and its surroundings and the people who would use it. Men with real talent as designers—such as A. H. Macmurdo, C. R. Mackintosh and Charles Voysey—began to work on furniture once again. They totally rejected the clutter of the Victorian sitting room in which every surface was decorated, every flat space bore a knick-knack of some kind. What really astonishes one about the interior designs of Mackintosh, for example, is their remarkable simplicity; a room is designed as a whole (just as Kent and Adam did) and the maximum use is made of the space available.

A fine-quality Charles II carved and giltwood mirror. About 1670.
Asprey & Co. Ltd.

A George I burr walnut bureau case. About 1720.
Glaisher & Nash Ltd.

A fine breakfront bookcase in the Hepplewhite manner. The body is in mahogany and cross-banded in kingwood. Made about 1785.
Asprey & Co. Ltd.

*A Georgian mahogany two-pillar dining table with swivel
action to one pedestal to support one leaf.*
Prides of London Ltd.

*A Regency mahogany
revolving bookcase resting on
a drum table. The lower legs
are inlaid with rosewood.*
Christie, Manson & Woods Ltd.

*A delightful dwarf bookcase
in rosewood cross-banded in
satinwood. About 1795.*
Glaisher & Nash Ltd.

A Regency painted open armchair. The upper back panel is painted with cupids en grisaille, flanked by carved lion heads. The open scroll arms rest on turned shaped legs.

Christie, Manson & Woods Ltd.

A George III mahogany chair in the Hepplewhite style. The seat is striped horsehair.

Christie, Manson & Woods Ltd.

A George II mahogany chair with stuffed back and covered with mid-eighteenth century Soho tapestry.

Christie, Manson & Woods Ltd.

Mallett & Sons (Antiques) Ltd.

Prides of London Ltd.

Mallett & Sons (Antiques) Ltd.

Top left: *a Windsor chair in yew and designed in the Gothic style. Mid-eighteenth century.*
Top right: *late eighteenth-century porter's chair in studded leather.*
Bottom left: *a Hepplewhite tub wing chair.*

109

A George III carved mahogany love seat of serpentine design. It is covered in red leather.

Christie, Manson & Woods Ltd.

A Sheraton inlaid mahogany sideboard.

Prides of London Ltd.

A George III rosewood and inlaid card table in the Sheraton style. It is inlaid with satinwood lines.

Christie, Manson & Woods Ltd.

Top left: *late seventeenth century Coromandel lacquer cabinet on richly carved stand.*
Top right: *Regency mahogany console table inlaid with brass.*
Left: *George II mahogany side table in style of Giles Grendey.*

111

A Regency card table inlaid in brass.
Prides of London Ltd.

A Regency rosewood sewing table.
Prides of London Ltd.

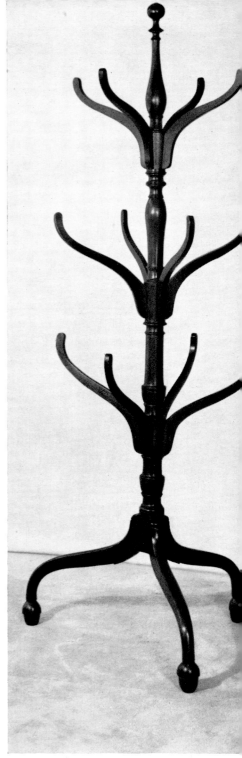

A Hepplewhite style mahogany hat stand.
Prides of London Ltd.

Left: *a mahogany cabinet inlaid with ivory and various woods. Made by Edwards and Roberts, 1891.*

Below: *an ebony cabinet and stand with Wedgwood plaques and gilt mounts. Made by Holland & Sons for the 1855 Paris Exhibition.*
Victoria & Albert Museum.

Balance wheel lantern clock by Thos Knifton at Ye Cross Keys in Lothbury. Early seventeenth century.
Science Museum, London.

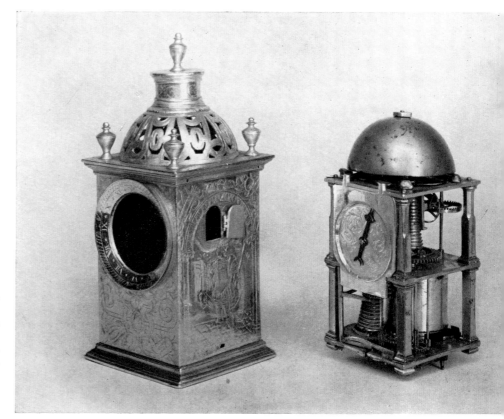

Vertical table clock by Bartholomew Newsam. c. 1590 and an early example of an English clock. The hinged door on the side is for inspecting the clock to see if it needs rewinding.
British Museum.

CLOCKS

Although we have no documentary evidence it is reasonable to suppose that primitive man divided time into the simple units of darkness and light. The year was an equally simple division based on such key events as seed planting, harvesting, migration of food animals and the like. The earliest method of telling time was by means of a sun-dial, the earliest recorded forms of which were used by the ancient Egyptians. They also used a 'clepsydra', a water-clock which measured time by the quantity of water discharged through a small opening in the body of the clepsydra. Also in use at about the same time was the sand-glass, the equivalent to our modern egg-timer. For some thousand years these three forms were the only means of telling time.

Although there are no detailed written records of the first mechanical clock, it is safe to assume that it was well established before 1350; in fact, Giovanni di Dondi of Padua described a planetarium operated by clockwork which he made during the period 1346–1364. Further, fourteenth century records tend to accept the clock as a common-place object.

So far as the actual timekeeping qualities of these early clocks are concerned they were no real improvement; in fact, it was necessary to check daily against a sundial. At this period the clock was used to announce the times of the masses. It is probable that such clocks had a primitive form of alarm to signal the ringing of a bell by a sacristan. Clocks were, naturally, built for secular purposes and usually were housed in a town hall or specially built tower. Needless to say there was great prestige in possessing a town clock. Some of the clocks told more than the time. They indicated the position of the heavenly bodies and the important days in the Church calendar. The oldest known clock of this period in England is that at Salisbury Cathedral (c. 1386) which was reconstructed to very near its original form in 1956.

It is natural to expect that as soon as the tower or turret clock had been established there would rise a need for smaller versions. This in fact happened in the fifteenth century. It is interesting to note that up to this time clockmaking was an aspect of the blacksmith's craft, but with the need for much smaller components it became a craft of the locksmith.

The domestic clock was weight driven like its larger counterpart and showed no great difference in its mechanism. It was usual to add an extra wheel to each train to enable the clock to run with a proportionally shorter fall for the weight so that the clock could hang at a convenient height for its dial to be seen. In the case of turret clocks, the weights would run down a tower and it was not of great importance to limit their fall. Even so, the early domestic clocks would need winding every twelve to fifteen hours. The accuracy of the clock would have shown no improvement over that of its larger predecessor.

The weight driven chamber clock appeared about the end of the fourteenth century and was made with little modification until the mid-seventeenth. France, Germany and Italy produced the best known examples, and other countries such as Switzerland also made these clocks, but not in such great numbers. Some of these early clocks were fitted with alarms and would be useful to arouse their owners from sleep. The clocks were not readily portable and would therefore have to be hung in the bedchamber, which limited their usefulness during the day. By this time the fashion of sleeping in a separate room would have become the accepted practice, and a portable timekeeper would have been extremely useful. The main difficulty was the weight drive.

The problem was solved by using a steel coiled spring as motive power instead of a weight. It was formerly believed that the spring came into use about 1500, but is now put as early as 1407. There were two main difficulties in the application of the mainspring. The first was the making of the spring itself. In those days steel was only capable of being produced in small quantities and the quality could not be guaranteed. The second difficulty was that a spring exerts

a greater force when it is wound up than when it is nearly run down, and with the verge escapement this is fatal for timekeeping. It was necessary, therefore, to provide some device to equalise the pull of the spring to get as nearly as possible a constant driving force. This was done by means of a fusee.

The spring driven clock was intended to stand on a table, and as it would be nearer to the person who wished to look at it it was possible to make the dial smaller than before. As time went on, smaller clocks began to be made, and by the early sixteenth century they were small enough to be carried on the person, and so the watch came into being.

Table clocks could be divided broadly into two groups, those with vertical and those with horizontal dials. The horizontal dial group developed into the early watches. As the sixteenth century progressed, table clocks acquired astronomical and other subsidiary dials. France, Germany and Italy supplied the bulk of these clocks; Augsburg and Nuremberg becoming celebrated for their clocks. The table clock marked a definite break with tradition in that the mechanism

The movement of a late seventeenth century clock, long case. Made by Jas. Clowes.

S. G. Edgcombe.

became boxed in; i.e., the clock had a case. The early wall clocks consisted simply of the mechanism with a little decoration, and the movement of the wheels could be seen.

As far as can be ascertained there were no British craftsmen capable of making a clock until the late sixteenth century. If any church or town desired a clock, the workmen had to come from abroad. Edward III granted a charter of protection to three 'Orologiers' in 1368, one of them coming from Delft, and they were allowed to exercise their craft in the realm. They probably worked on clocks for the King at Westminster, Queensborough, and Langley about this period, and the clocks at Salisbury and Wells have also been attributed to them.

Repairers of clocks were known in Britain from the middle ages and references to them all seem to indicate that they were working on turret clocks, but it is doubtful if any of them were English. For instance there is a reference to 'Roger the Clockmaker' being sent from Barnstaple when Exeter Cathedral clock needed repair in 1424, and the 'clokke maker of Kolcester' (Colchester), repaired a clock for the Duke of Norfolk in 1483. The word 'make' was at that time synonymous with 'mend', so it cannot be assumed that these 'clockmakers' actually made clocks or did anything else than repair or maintain existing clocks. Henry VIII possessed a number of clocks and watches, all of which must have been imported from the Continent or made by visiting workmen. Elizabeth I also owned many clocks and watches and had her own clockmaker in the person of Nicholas Urseau who was of French descent, but her clock keeper was Bartholomew Newsam who received the office of clockmaker in 1590 on the death of Urseau, and thus became the first English Royal Clockmaker. Newsam is believed to have been a Yorkshireman.

Mention should also be made of Randolph Bull who made the clockwork for Thomas Dallam's organ which was presented by Queen Elizabeth I to the Sultan of Turkey in 1599. Bull later became Royal Clockmaker. Other names of British clockmakers begin to appear about this time, indicating the establishment of the craft.

The style that emerged is popularly known as the 'Lantern' clock, but is also known as 'Cromwellian' or 'Bedpost' and by various other names. Late examples in which the dial is much wider than the movement are called 'Sheepshead'. The movement of these clocks was basically the weight driven wall clock of the Continent, but most of the metal used was brass and the clock was generally not placed so high. A wheel balance was always used. So far no evidence has been forthcoming of an English Lantern clock with a foliot. The design would not allow for this, as the bell was not very far from the top plate of the movement, and was flanked on three sides by frets which would have rendered the adjustment of the small weights difficult. Regulation of a Lantern clock would always have been carried out by increasing or decreasing the amount of lead shot carried in a hollow on top of the going weight, and thereby altering the amount of driving force available.

The Lantern clock had a very long life. It began in the reign of Elizabeth I and continued to be made until that of George III, although by this time it was only being made in the provinces.

The Lantern clock at first had a narrow chapter ring with stumpy figures. The hour hand was of sturdy construction to permit of its being set to time, and the inner edge of the chapter ring was engraved with quarter marks to allow the time to be read with greater accuracy. As the seventeenth century progressed the dials became larger and the figures longer, and after the invention of the pendulum, minute hands were added. Smaller versions with an alarm only and no striking work were produced for travelling purposes. The popularity of the style lasted until long after they had ceased to be made as a regular item of the clockmaker's output. During the nineteenth century many old clocks had their movements replaced by contemporary spring driven ones and were adapted for standing on a mantelpiece, which is quite out of keeping with this type. Later still, small versions with platform escapements were sold for use on desks or bedside tables.

Any clocks produced in Britain before about 1600 had been made by foreigners, but as the native talent was developed a desire arose to eliminate competition from continental workmen, and accordingly the King was petitioned to establish a guild for the regulation of the clockmaker's craft in London. In 1631 the Clockmakers' Company was incorporated, and previously to this most of the clockmakers had belonged to the Blacksmiths' Company. The Clockmakers' Company controlled the training of future members of the craft, carefully limiting their numbers so that the market should not be flooded with clocks, but in spite of this London clockmakers were often guilty of having too many apprentices and were accordingly fined. The officers of the Company also had the right to search premises with a constable if it were suspected that watches and clocks of poor quality were to be found there, and if such things were found, the Company had the right to order their destruction.

By the middle of the seventeenth century clockmaking had reached a comparatively high standard. Table clocks were being made with various astronomical indicators, and their movements included parts made of brass and were finely made. The weight-driven wall clock became refined into the Lantern clock in England and in other countries it was subjected to improvements and new forms of decoration. The only disadvantage was that all instruments of this period were shocking timekeepers. Errors of a quarter of an hour to an hour a day could be expected, and a clock that gained one day might lose the next. Great efforts were made to correct this, the most successful being the pendulum.

The Italian scientist Galileo (1564–1642) is reputed to have noticed that the swinging lamps in the Cathedral at Pisa took the same time to perform each swing whether swinging a wide or narrow arc. Near the end of his life he dictated to his son a description of a timekeeper controlled by a pendulum. The son began work on a model of this timekeeper but left it incomplete at his death in 1649. A German clockmaker, Johann Phillip Treffler, was also thinking of a pendulum as a time measurer, and made a clock for the Medici Palace in Florence. The name that will always be associated with the use of the pendulum to control a clock is that of Christiaan Huygens (1629–95), the Dutch physicist, Huygens made his experimental model on Christmas Day 1656 and obtained a patent in 1657. He commissioned a clockmaker in The Hague, Salomon Coster, to produce the clocks, and Coster turned out some excellent work incorporating the new principle.

The early pendulum clocks broke completely new ground in clock design. These clocks were so far ahead of their time that until recently many people regarded them as Victorian. Most noticeable outwardly was the use of a wooden case, which was almost unknown at the time, while internally there was the pendulum itself and also the use of a direct drive from the mainspring without the use of a fusee. Apparently such confidence was felt in the new controller that it was not considered necessary to modify the force of the mainspring. The movement was virtually that of a table clock turned on its side, while the pendulum was very short, as the verge escapement was retained, involving the pendulum swinging through a wide arc. It was now at long last worthwhile to fit a hand indicating minutes.

As soon as the invention of the pendulum became known in England, John Fromanteel, a member of a family of clockmakers of Dutch descent living in London, went to work for Coster to learn how the new sort of clock was made. An invention that brought the accuracy of a clock within a few minutes per day was something that would be eagerly sought after by every clockmaker. By 1658 the making of pendulum clocks was being advertised in the 'Commonwealth Mercury' by Ahasuerus Fromanteel, another member of the family.

The introduction of the pendulum into clockwork marked the beginning of the period of almost two centuries during which the London makers led the world in craftsmanship and invention. Not until the mid-nineteenth century, when the London makers refused to move with the times, was that supremacy lost. The restoration of the Monarchy in 1660 meant the end of the period of austerity enforced by the Commonwealth, and the people were ready to spend money to re-furnish their homes in the latest style. We find at this period that architectural designs in ebony were the fashion for clock cases, and British makers quickly abandoned two of the main features of the Dutch clocks. They connected the pendulum directly to the verge, doing away with the separate suspension and the cheeks in one blow, and they also did away with the velvet ground to the dial, preferring matted brass or later plain brass engraved and spandrels made of cast brass applied separately.

Development in the late seventeenth century was rapid. The severely architectural styles of the sixties evolved into the basket top of the sixteen-eighties. Ebony remained a favourite wood for cases, but clocks tended to get taller as the century progressed, and movements became technically more refined. No record of this period would be complete without mentioning the name of Thomas Tompion. He acquired the title of 'The Father of English Watchmaking', and was buried in Westminster Abbey. Six thousand watches and five hundred and fifty clocks by him have been listed, which means that he could not have made them all with his own hands. Such production could not be achieved without a large staff of skilled workmen, and it is perhaps as the first 'production engineer' rather than as an horologist that Tompion ought to be remembered. Rumour has it that he established a workshop at Aldgate outside the City limits in order to escape the jurisdiction of the Clockmakers' Company. His official premises and residence was at Water Lane, Blackfriars, near Fleet Street.

Neither Tompion nor any of his contemporaries made their own dials or cases, each being provided by skilled engravers or cabinet makers. The name of the 'clockmaker' on the dial indicated the man who supervised the production of the clock and not the man who actually made it. As time progressed, we find specialist workshops producing movements for more than one celebrated maker who would willingly put his name on the dial as if the work had been his. He took the responsibility for the finished article, but was maker in name only.

The usual English name for spring driven pendulum clocks of the seventeenth and eighteenth centuries was 'Bracket Clocks'. These clocks were not usually placed on brackets, which implies a permanent home, but were rather intended to be carried from room to room and were even provided with a carrying handle for this purpose. Many of these clocks had no striking mechanism but were provided with a cord which could be pulled to make the clock repeat hours and quarters; a very useful feature when the clock stood on a bedside table during the night. The term 'Table Clock' would be far more appropriate for these clocks, but as it has already been used for the earlier metal cased clocks, 'Bracket Clock' will have to stand.

The advent of the pendulum not only led to a development of the spring clock as first created by Coster, but also produced an entirely new design of clock. The old clocks with foliot or wheel balance would have needed winding every twelve to fifteen hours and at the same time it would be necessary to regulate them every day after comparison with a sundial. Most public clocks had a sundial nearby for this purpose. After the clock had been made so accurate that the daily regulation was no longer necessary, there was an incentive to prolong the intervals between winding. Spring-driven pendulum clocks in their early days were made to run for one day, then two or more and finally eight days between windings. During the early years of the reign of Charles II, London makers evolved a new type of clock which would run for eight days. The movement was generally similar to that of the spring clock except that the drive was by weights supported by catgut lines which were wound round brass barrels, and the clock was wound by means of a key through the dial as were the spring clocks. The short pendulum was retained as the verge was still the only available escapement. The ebony architectural case was provided but the clock was intended to be hung on the wall. The Dutch spring clocks were usually provided with means for hanging them on the wall as well as feet for standing on a table, but spring clocks in England were seldom seen with this feature. The exposed weights of the new type of clock were provided with polished brass containers, but even so they were considered unsightly and clocks were produced with a long tall cupboard below them to hide the weights from view. The next step was to make the cupboard and the top into a free standing unit and the 'Long Case' clock was born. (It is more popularly known as the 'Grandfather clock'.)

The earliest were quite small, being only about five feet high, and the ebony architectural style was used for the cases. The Fromanteel family was associated with this type in the early days. The movements were closely allied to the pendulum controlled spring clocks which were being produced and which were direct descendants of the Table clocks. The Long-case clock is therefore more closely connected with the Table clock than with the weight driven wall clock.

The advantages of a longer pendulum were being considered at this period as it would be more capable of receiving fine adjustments in length and therefore the regulation of the clock would be more exact. By having fewer beats per hour fewer teeth would be necessary in the wheels, thereby saving labour.

There has been a lot of discussion on the subject of whether Robert Hooke or William Clement, a London clockmaker, was the inventor of the anchor escapement. A very strong point in Clement's favour is that he was originally an anchor smith, and the shape of the anchors on which he worked no doubt suggested the escapement; as well as making clocks with a pendulum five feet long beating a second and a quarter. These early clocks had cases very little larger than the short pendulum type, but as the century progressed there was a tendency for the Long-case clock to get bigger, especially when examples were produced which ran for one, three or six months between windings. The earliest clocks with a very long period of running were three made by Tompion in 1676 for Greenwich Observatory. These clocks were intended to be wound only once a year.

The Long-case clock rapidly became popular after the invention of the anchor escapement. The cases at first had an ebony finish and later marquetry and parquetry became popular, while in the eighteenth century lacquered cases were fashionable. In the early part of the same century walnut also occurs, and once mahogany had established itself its popularity lasted until the end of the English Long-case clock in the nineteenth century.

The Lantern clock was still being made in the eighteenth century, but many movements of the Lantern type were also being produced with square brass dials intended to be covered by a hood and hung on the wall, or else to be fitted in a country version of the Long case. One encounters many of these one-handed clocks in a variety of cases not always pleasing to the eye, and in many cases a minute hand has been added. This can always be detected when the old dial is retained, for the original dial has quarter hour marks inside the hour figures and no minute marks outside them. Some of these clocks have movements with the wheels held between two brass plates as on the eight-day clocks, but they are still to be considered as belonging to the Lantern family. In their final form down to about 1850 they were produced in Birmingham with the usual painted iron dials found on nineteenth-century clocks. By this time most of the eight-day movements and dials were being produced there, with the name of the vendor painted on the dial to order, and the cases would be made to the order of the purchaser in his own locality.

As the Long-case clock increased in size, the dial tended to increase also. Beginning with a size of about nine inches square immediately after the Restoration, dials had increased to twelve inches square by about 1690, and early in the eighteenth century an arch was placed above the square dial. Early arches were made separately, but soon the dial and arch were being made in one piece. One of the earliest arch dials is to be found on the Tompion clock in the Pump Room at Bath. Dials at this period were made of sheet brass with silvered chapter rings and cast spandrels fitted separately, but as the eighteenth century progressed some dials were made with the figures engraved directly on to the dial itself, or else the dial was silvered all over and the figures were indicated in black. This led the way to the painted iron dials characteristic of the late eighteenth and early nineteenth centuries.

As soon as the arch was added to the dial it became a space that needed filling. Sometimes a plaque with the maker's name and place of business was put there, or a strike/silent hand would occupy that position. After about 1730 the phases of the moon were indicated by a disc bearing two moons that rotated once in two lunations, and this neatly filled the space in the arch. The square dial was mostly used on the thirty-hour Lantern type movements, but had a longer life on eight-day clocks in Lancashire and Wales where it would sometimes include moonphases in an opening below the figure XII. To know the phase of the moon was of great importance in the eighteenth century, as only at the time of full moon was it possible to go out at night. Moon dials often include an indicator to show high tide at a certain port, but this has to be specially calibrated for the place in question and is of no use elsewhere.

The day of the month was indicated at first by a figure showing through a square opening above figure VI. Later a dial was placed here or a kidney shaped slot allowed figures on a disc to be visible. The seconds hand placed below figure XII goes back to the early days of the anchor escapement, for with a pendulum beating seconds and a scapewheel of thirty teeth the division of the minute can be indicated on the dial with very little extra trouble. The eight-day clock is recognisable at a glance by the winding holes in the dial, but even this can prove a trap for the unwary. Less fortunate people who could not afford an eight-day clock would sometimes have false winding holes painted on the dial of their clock to give the impression that it was an eight-day one when in fact it was only a thirty-hour clock and would be wound by pulling the chain or rope inside the trunk.

The Long-case clock became particularly associated with England. The only other country that took it seriously was Holland, and tradition was still strong enough to keep it popular in the U.S.A. after 1776, although native American styles drove it off the market there before it had disappeared in England. In the latter country, its popularity in London waned during the later part of the eighteenth century, but it was still popular in the provinces, particularly in the north, and the mill owners made rich by the Industrial Revolution always desired very flamboyant styles for their homes, helping to create distinctive types for Lancashire and Yorkshire as the eighteenth century gave way to the nineteenth. The type was also popular in Wales and Scotland.

This is, of course, only the briefest survey, and those readers who are particularly interested in the evolution and mechanical principles of clock movements should refer to such books as E. J. Tyler's 'European Clocks' and/or J. D. Robertson's 'The Evolution of Clockwork'. Other useful books are listed in the booklist at the end of this book.

Rear view of a lantern clock by
William Bowyer (1626–47) showing
the construction and arrangement
of the mechanism of a lantern
clock of this period.

S. G. Edgcombe.

Great Chamber clock by
William Bowyer (1626–47).
The name is
engraved on the
front of the dial.

S. G. Edgcombe.

A small travelling alarm clock of the 'lantern' type. The inscription gives the maker's name and place. It can be dated early eighteenth century.

S. G. Edgcombe.

English spring-driven pendulum clock and a very early specimen.

British Museum.

A bracket clock with time strike alarm and day of month. It was made by James Markwick of London, and signed 'Jacobus', c. 1670.

S. G. Edgcombe.

An architectural bracket clock made by Edward East, London, 1660–70. The maker's name is engraved on the face and the day of the month window is situated just below the numeral XII.

P. G. Dawson.

A late seventeenth-century bracket clock made by de Charme. The square dial is decorated with cherub head spandrels.

P. G. Dawson.

An early nineteenth-century Regency bracket clock.

S. G. Edgcombe.

Left: *a month long-case clock made by David Guepin, London. c. 1690. Note the beautifully finished marquetry case.*
Centre: *a quarter chiming long-case clock made by Henry Jones, London. c. 1690.*
Right: *a long-case clock made by George Graham, London, about 1730–40.*

S. G. Edgcombe.

Left: *a long-case clock in mahogany. Made by Joseph Stevens about 1780.*
Right: *a long-case clock made by Chime of Sheffield and dated about 1820.*

P. G. Dawson.

*A Gothic style clock made by
James Garland, London, about 1820.*
S. G. Edgcombe.

*A long-case clock made by
Nicholas Lambert (1750–70).*
Uhrenmuseum der Stadt, Wien.

*An early nineteenth-century
English dial clock. Made by John
Grant, Fleet Street.*
P. G. Dawson.

A cane basket of cotton flowers under a protective glass dome; a typical example of Victoriana.
Redmond Phillips.

A pierced Hinton bowl with a selection of wax and glass fruits. Such arrangements graced many a Victorian drawing room.
Lionel Young Antiques.

VICTORIANA

Many people are still unable even to hear the word 'Victoriana' without a look of distaste crossing their faces; and it will probably always be so. We became accustomed for a time to being told that men always despised the work of their fathers, found the work of their grandfathers quaint, but never spared themselves in their admiration for their great-grandfathers. It was to be merely a matter of time before we all sighed with pleasure at the sight of a Victorian armchair or a piece of press-moulded glass, and sentimental china figures and Valentines would soon have us clapping our hands with delight. To a certain extent this has happened. People now spend a great deal of money on collecting Victoriana, but they are different people from those who still follow the tastes of the eighteenth century. The two ages are as far apart in their attitudes to domestic decoration as they have ever been, and it will probably always be so, for the machine age destroyed all continuity in the spheres that it was able to affect. One can only appreciate Victoriana, then, by taking a quite different attitude to it, and this is what the antique dealers and their customers are learning to do. And that attitude involves thinking of each object as a manifestation of the period that produced it, not evaluating it according to how it has managed to combine functionalism and beauty. Those who find little to appreciate in the life-cycle of the average Victorian are bound to remain cold to the charms of Victorian period flavour.

We are not talking here of the fine arts during the Victorian period, nor of those restless spirits who found the Victorian way of life quite as repulsive as its detractors of today and who worked towards a new order, in the arts as well as in society in general. It would be wrong to put the Victoriana label on the work of the Pre-Raphaelites, who had this, if nothing else, in common with other artistic movements, that they were trying to do something new. Wrong, too, to put such a label on the work of the great Victorian designers—William Morris, C. R. Mackintosh, Christopher Dresser—who, more or less, escaped from their own age.

We may set the tone by starting with the Valentine. In the 18th century this had been a hand-written affair, decorated by the hand of the suitor, but the Victorians took advantage not only of etching and lithography, but also of all kinds of outlandish techniques and materials for decorating these mass-produced cards—simulated flowers, paper-lace and ribbons, paper cut in Gothic patterns and coloured gold or silver, shells and feathers. A favourite topic was a card of a Church door or window—extravagantly Gothic, of course, which opened to reveal a marriage ceremony in progress, and was captioned with some commonplace verses:

> *May thy bosom thus incline—*
> *To a faithful heart like mine,*
> *Ever loving—ever true—*
> *A counterpart—my love of you.*

Another one was the 'marriage nest', depicted

as just that: a rustic thatched cottage perched in a bird's nest, surrounded by flowers and foliage. Others took themselves less seriously, and went so far as to send humorous Valentines: Valentines in the form of banknotes for example, drawn on the 'Lover's Banking Company', and promising to pay on demand the entire love of 'the suppliant who sends this'. They were so similar, in many cases, to real banknotes, that they eventually had to be prohibited. The bill was a popular one too: the sender would demand payment of 300 kisses for 'compensation for doctor's bills, palpitation of the heart, giddiness, etc.'

The Valentine eventually had to give way in face of the Christmas card, however; a much more commercial venture, for though a few reckless gentlemen might send more than one Valentine, everybody could send large numbers of Christmas cards. In fact, social pressures made it compulsory for them to do so. The early Christmas cards—they were becoming really popular by the 1870s —followed the designs of the Valentines with plenty of paper-lace and tinsel. Later, Christmas gathered around it its own motifs: robins, berries, holly, snow, bonneted ladies stepping from coaches into the snow to greet their friends on the festive day. Some of the better known Victorian designers applied themselves to Christmas cards. Walter Crane produced some delightful, flowing Art Nouveau designs, and Kate Greenaway made cards and calendars with precocious little girls in long frocks and beribboned hats dancing round the borders.

For period flavour, there is nothing to better the Victorian photograph. The daguerrotype process was becoming known at the very beginning of Victoria's reign, and at the same time W. H. Fox Talbot was conducting the experiments that led him to the production of the calotype, the first of the negative-positive processes. But, throughout the period, photography remained a very complicated business requiring a very great deal of cumbersome equipment, and a considerable amount of patience in the sitters,

who had to pose for long periods before the camera without moving. It is partly this that gives Victorian photographs their characteristic appearance: the look of frozen immobility in the faces and the staring eyes. A great deal of pleasure can be obtained from the family photographs—the portraits of Papa surrounded by his flock, and the children dressed up to the nines and caught in an heroic pose. The work of the top photographers is rarer, of course, but well worth looking at. Considering the unwieldy technical processes they had to struggle with, these early photographers achieved some remarkable results. Outstanding among them was David Octavius Hill, the Scottish painter, and R. Adamson, who used the calotype process in its early days. Their picture of *Elizabeth Johnstone, the beauty of Newhaven*, taken in 1848, is one of the great classics of photography, the subject strikingly portrayed in broad masses of black and white, with the minimum of detail. Their photographs are necessarily stiff, but even at this early stage they began to see that photography could be used in a quite different manner from paint and canvas, as they showed in intimate pictures like *Girls at a bird-cage*. Julia Margaret Cameron came a little later, and worked primarily as a portrait photographer, but also tried to experiment in new fields, not always with success. Her photographic illustrations to Tennyson's *Idylls of the King*, for example, are cluttered with unconvincingly faked scenery and too many actors looking uncomfortable in unlikely costumes. Yet, in other 'literary' pictures she achieved great effects with photographs in which the subjects were in full focus while the less relevant parts of the scene remained slightly blurred. She seems to have been genuinely inspired by the sad, pre-Raphaelite face of her maid, Mary Hillier, whom she frequently used as her model in anecdotal photographs; *The Angel at the Sepulchre*, for example, is a striking, even if not very photographic, print.

We may take, for a moment, a diversion into the nursery and look at the juvenile drama, a curious development of the tinsel pictures of popular actors that were sold in the early part of the 19th century for the delight of adults. Sheets of paper were sold, either 'penny plain or twopence coloured', on which were depicted the actors and scenes from some choice stage production of the time. These could be cut out—and, if necessary, coloured—and mounted on cardboard. The scenes are done with all the exaggeration of a pantomime set, while the figures take up the most extraordinarily stiff poses, usually with the right leg straight out and left knee slightly bent. Character is revealed by means of the clothes and by highly formalised hand and arm gestures, the faces usually being completely expressionless. Also in the nursery are some much sought-after toys. The better doll's houses are probably the best record we have of the appearance of a room in an ordinary Victorian house, for the wallpaper, curtains and upholstery fabrics, chair, table and bed designs are all authentic and down to scale, even including pictures on the walls, decorative pottery and cooking pots. The life outside is also recorded in the most remarkable detail—carts, carriages, trains and animals. The sophisticated child might have a clockwork automaton combined with a musical box—though it would probably have been made in Germany—or a pair of clowns who could be made to tumble slowly down stairs over each other's backs by the ingenious contrivance of joining them with mercury-filled rods. The Victorian middle classes were also quite as keen on 'educative' toys as their 20th century successors, though they were less subtle in their approach. Thus jig-saw puzzles would be used to explain the uses to which domestic animals could be put.

The fittings of the Victorian house—notably the oil lamps—have now become fashionable, so much so that it even seems to be worth the trouble of reproducing them. As Victorian houses are modernised it may be possible to obtain some of the more permanent fittings, such as lavatories, which were profusely covered with Gothic decora-

tion, or other fashionable motifs. The bathroom began its career late in Victorian days, and it seems unlikely that many genuine Victorian bathrooms remain, but one can still find the movable fittings, such as the ewer and basin, and the chamber-pot. All kinds of external decorations for the house can be obtained from demolition contractors, and this was a field in which the Victorians achieved some good effects. There are cast-iron balconies and pleasant cast-iron street

Highly-decorated Victorian oil-lamp.
David Drummond.

lamp brackets for suspending above door-ways. A great improvement can be made in the fireplaces of Victorian houses if the correct cast-iron grate and decorative sur-round is installed.

Reverting to our theme of period flavour, we would do well to mention the Victorian poster. The posters for Victorian melodramas speak eloquently—as the plays themselves did, in a rather crude form—of Victorian attitudes, especially moral attitudes. The stock-in-trade of these melodramas—the unfaithful wives, the evicting landlords, the distraught heroine, and the hero who mis-takenly believes himself to have been guilty of a hideous crime—varied but a little, like the characters in a pantomime, requiring only a little rearrangement. The posters were not always pictorial; sometimes they are purely typographical, the title and the main characters being in huge, black letters, some-times aligned rather drunkenly on the page. But the designers of pictorial posters had a rich field of choice in their search for macabre illustrations. Oddly enough, in view of this, their products are frequently lifeless, like the characters in the juvenile drama; the actors are shown in entirely conventional poses, with the hero or the detective stretching out his arm in accusation, and the villain shrinking back, non-plussed. Towards the end of the century, however, the role of the poster began to change entirely, and it became an acceptable art form. In France, this change will always be associated with the name of Toulouse-Lautrec, but the same wind of change was blowing in England too, where D'Oyly Carte, the head of the opera company that performed the works of Gilbert and Sullivan, decided to encourage better poster design in England by attaching an artist to his Savoy Theatre as their regular poster designer. The artist he chose was the talented Dudley Hardy, whose work showed the strong influence of Art Nouveau ideas in design, especially in his use of large areas of flat pattern, and tortuous, flowing lines. This kind of work, as well as the strikingly mem-orable designs of Aubrey Beardsley, affected not only the design of theatre posters, but all kinds of advertisements. Advertisements for the most ordinary objects might contain, as their centrepiece, an Art Nouveau maiden with a long, swirling train, as if she were wearing a wedding dress. But with this we are moving into the twentieth century, at least in spirit.

'Books' are dealt with elsewhere in this work as a general topic, but the Victorian illustrated books and magazines had a character all of their own and are an ex-cellent field for those who find them attrac-tive, for there is still so much available. The standard vehicle for the illustrator from the late 1850s almost until the end of the century was the wood engraving, and this medium was used in such a spate of fine illustrations in the 1860s that 'the illustrators of the Sixties' has become an acceptable chapter heading for a remarkable period of art history. Some of the illustrations to the greater Victorian novels have never been properly superseded, so that George Cruik-shank's illustrations for *Oliver Twist* are still familiar to children today, and have become an almost essential part of the book. Phiz (whose real name was H. K. Brown) did some equally memorable illustrations to Dickens, as well as others for the less known novels of Lever and Ainsworth. Our im-pressions of Alice and the White Rabbit are still formed from the drawings of Sir John Tenniel, engraved by the outstanding Brothers Dalziel; and Kate Greenaway's books of poems and drawings of children continue to be printed without a change. In-deed, the Victorian children's book was very highly regarded by artists, and gave rise to Randolph Caldecott's Picture Books, and attracted Walter Crane, who later made such a great impact in the field of design, especially Art Nouveau design. Crane shared many things in common with William Morris, who probably produced the finest of all Victorian books at his Kelmscott Press. In book design, as in other things, Morris began with first principles; he designed his own type and used the finest materials for his paper. Each double page he considered as a thing to be designed on its own, and so he enclosed within borders of convoluting leaves and flowers and drawings of Burne-Jones and the text in his new type. But again, we are straying from what is strikingly Victorian. Far more so among books, are those filled with the luminous colour illustrations of Miles Birket Foster, perhaps the 'prettiest' of Victorian painters. We may also mention some of the cartoonists of the Victorian period. We have already referred to John Tenniel as a book illustrator, but he was also the chief cartoonist of *Punch* for a long time. George du Maurier quietly satirised the life and fashions of the Victorian middle classes in such a way that they themselves could smile at them, while Charles Keen drew some rather more hot-blooded cartoons of life among the ordinary people of his generation. Phil May, who drew for *Punch* towards the end of the century characterised the same kind of people but in a simpler and very pleasing style, obtaining strong effect from a few well-chosen lines.

Glass oil-lamp decorated with traditional snow scene.
John Hall.

A stove in cast bronze and brass with panels of earthenware.
Victoria & Albert Museum.

A needlework picture depicting a scene from Sir Walter Scott's novel The Talisman. It was made about 1860.
Victoria & Albert Museum.

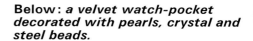

Left: *a tinsel picture of Richard Coeur de Lion on a printed background.*

Below: *a velvet watch-pocket decorated with pearls, crystal and steel beads.*

A typical Victorian Valentine card. The edges were gilded with silver leaves and branches. Birds, usually making a nest, were a feature of such cards.
London Museum.

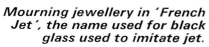

Mourning jewellery in 'French Jet', the name used for black glass used to imitate jet.
Cameo Corner.

A hand-painted Christmas card. The surround is a fine quality paper lace.

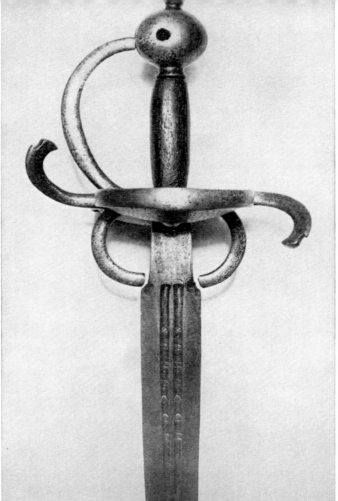

The hilt end of a late sixteenth-century sword. It bears the name of the famous Spanish maker SAHAGOM but this was frequently counterfeited.

L. Gibson.

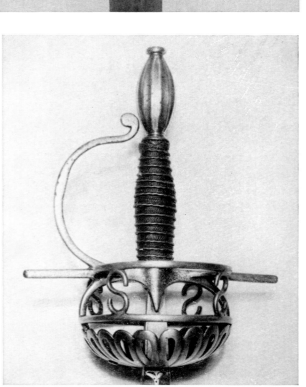

Left: *a dagger with an agate grip and silver quillons. Probably Scottish and early seventeenth-century.*
Right: *an English dagger with burr walnut grip with silver mounds and quillons.*

E. Perry.

Hilt of an English rapier of about 1620; blade length 43½ inches.

L. Gibson.

EDGED
WEAPONS

Some edged weapons have certain national characteristics, but even these are blurred by the fact that fashions were copied and thus a sword with an apparently typical German look may, in fact, have been made in England. Dating too must always be general rather than specific, for many swords continued in use long after a new style had been introduced, and indeed not only were they in use but were still in production.

The history of the sword has been largely influenced by its manner of use: it may be intended primarily for thrusting, in which case, length of blade, rigidity and the point are of prime importance, but if it is intended for slashing, the edge is then of prime concern. Most swords have in fact been cut and thrust in that they could be used for both purposes, but in this case some compromise, as far as design is concerned, had to be effected. Again, the shape and size of the sword depended on whether it was for infantry or cavalry, and although it was generally discarded as an infantry weapon during the eighteenth century the cavalry continued to use it until they were, in turn, made obsolete. Even at the end of its useful life controversy still raged as to whether the cavalry sword was a slashing or a stabbing weapon.

Saxon and Viking swords were basically the same in design and detail but they are not common, for the great majority of grave burials lack swords, although most have spears or the smaller knife weapon called a *seax*, *sax* or *scramasax*. These weapons range in length from six to thirty inches, but all are single edged with an acutely sloping point and they were obviously intended as a general purpose knife as well as a slashing weapon and were carried in a sheath suspended from a waist belt.

Some of these weapons are finely inlaid with many styles and forms of decoration. Surviving swords are most frequently straight bladed, double edged, thirty to forty inches in length and with little or no point, clearly indicating that they were primarily slashing weapons. Most of these and later swords have one or more grooves cut into the blade and these are often erroneously described as blood gutters, but they are in fact known as fullers after a groove cutting tool. They were intended to lighten the blade by removing some of the metal without sacrificing its rigidity and are found on sword blades of all periods.

In order to balance the blade and make it easier to wield the sword a counterbalance was fitted at the opposite end of the grip and this is known as the pommel. Early pommels were often just flat metal washers, but soon acquired a certain decorative quality. From about the ninth century the pommel was often made with the top edge divided into an odd number of lobes, but this style was out of favour by the eleventh century. Protection to the hand was afforded by a simple bar across the top of the blade—the quillons —which protected beyond the edge or shoulder of the blade.

The Normans who invaded England in

1066 were largely armed with a sword very similar to that of the Viking, although the quillons were rather larger and projected further out over the shoulder of the blade. Their pommels were of two main varieties—a brazil-nut shape, which was to remain in fashion until the latter part of the thirteenth century, and a roughly semi-circular or recumbent D-shape, which was to be discarded by the middle of the twelfth century.

About this same period a new shape of pommel became common, although it is known to have been used occasionally at least a century previously, and this round, wheel-pommel was to continue in use, with variations in detail, until the middle of the fifteenth century. At first it was flat, but at the turn of the century the edges were shaved back and by the middle of the century it had acquired two hub-like projections at the centre, but this style was discarded and by the middle of the fifteenth century a solid, flat-sided disc was in vogue. Although pommels were usually of metal, weapons of the highest quality were occasionally fitted with ones made of jasper and other mineral compounds.

Blades were gradually increased in length and towards the end of the thirteenth century sword lengths ranged from 45 to 55 inches, but at the same time blades were made narrower, often with inlaid inscriptions in brass or silver. Not only was the blade increased in length but the grip was correspondingly lengthened so that in normal use the weapon could be used in one hand, but there was room to grasp the hilt with both hands to deliver a far more powerful blow. Collectors refer to this intermediate size as a hand-and-a-half, or bastard, sword. As the grip was lengthened so too were the quillons, and although the great majority were still quite straight some were made which curved slightly towards the blade. This tendency to curve the quillons increased until, by the middle of the fifteenth century, the great majority had very pronounced downward curves.

Apart from the emphasised points, blades altered but little except in one respect and this change was occasioned by a variation in use, for it was becoming common practice to improve the grip on the sword by hooking the forefinger over one of the quillons. Thus, by the middle of the fourteenth century, some blades were made with the few inches of the edge situated just below the quillons left blunt and unsharpened, but this *ricasso* does not become really common until the sixteenth century. Following the appearance of the *ricasso* it was logical to add some form of protection for the finger and a small, hook-like bar was added below the quillon or, more rarely, the blade was actually shaped to accommodate the finger. Around the middle of the fifteenth century a similar ring was added on the other side of the blade and these two extra guards were known as the arms of the hilt.

During the fifteenth century the *estoc* was to become a very popular weapon. This was rather more of a short lance than a sword, for the blade was triangular or square in section and the weapon was designed solely for thrusting. *Estocs* were seldom used as the prime weapon except in foot combat at the lists, but books of the fifteenth century intended to instruct in all styles of combat, *Fechtbucher*, show how a combatant should use this type of weapon.

Two developments were taking place, probably in Italy, that were to affect the design of both hilt and blade in a most dramatic fashion. Sometime around 1480 one of the quillons was curved up towards the pommel to form a guard for the hand-knuckle bow, and at about the same period lugs on the quillons were extended until they united and formed a horizontal ring on the side. The hand was thus becoming enclosed within a series of protective loops and bars, and during the sixteenth century this tendency developed enormously. It has been pointed out that the improved armour had emphasised the need to thrust rather than slash and in Italy during the early part of the sixteenth century there was developed a style of sword play which was known as fencing. Masters set up schools to teach this new fashion in sword play which stressed not only the use of the point, but the use of the whole sword for defence as well as offence.

Fencing weapons were, at first, very long bladed, up to five feet in extreme cases, double edged with a short grip and a guard of loops and bars of varying complexity. This type, known as a rapier, first appears about 1530 and was probably of Spanish origin. Pommels on these weapons, indeed on the vast majority of swords from the sixteenth century onwards, were round or egg shaped. As rapiers were essentially civilian weapons they were consequently often of extremely fine quality and embellished with many forms of decoration—a few were even fitted with gold or enamelled hilts. About 1580 it became the fashion to cut or chisel the steel into high relief figures or patterns and much of this work is outstandingly good.

Military swords were not as elaborate as the civilian rapier having much simpler guards which lacked the intricate combination of bars and arms. Simple cross-like guards had gone out of style by the middle of the sixteenth century and in the latter part of the same century most swords had rings mounted on one or both sides of the quillons whilst others had solid shells. Quillons were also curved to greater or lesser degrees.

The complete antithesis of the light, flickering rapiers were the great two-handed swords which flourished during the sixteenth century, although they were mentioned as early as the middle of the fourteenth century. Especially popular in Northern Europe, they were used entirely as slashing weapons, being whirled round above the head. Most measure about six feet in length and weigh around eight pounds each—less than their size might lead one to expect. Many had that section of the blade below the quillons covered with leather and this enabled the user to grip the blade here and so effectively shorten the length of the weapon. Two hook-like lugs which project from the side of the blade just below this leather-covered sec-

tion act as quillons to guard the user's hand. Large two-handed swords were popular in Scotland and were known as great swords, *Claidheamh mor*, from which is derived the term Claymore. These rare weapons have straight, down-sloping quillons which usually terminate in pierced trefoils. Claymores of the seventeenth century commonly have a single shell on one side of the quillons.

During the seventeenth and eighteenth centuries frequent wars stimulated an increase in the number of swords produced and also the types available. Ever-changing tactics stimulated ideas about sword design and similarly new fencing styles were evolved which required different kinds of swords. It is during the second quarter of the seventeenth century that one very distinctive sword, the cup-hilt rapier, first appears and although it originated in Spain or Italy it was soon widely adopted. Elaborate bars, guards, counter-guards and shells were replaced by one fairly deep, rounded dish, often pierced or chiselled, with very long, thin quillons and knucklebow.

Somewhat similar in general appearance, although easily distinguished, is the dish rapier of the mid-seventeenth century, for the dish is far smaller and less deep than on Spanish weapons and there is no knucklebow.

In France during this period the fencing fashion required a shorter blade and by about 1630 a transitional rapier with two shells, no knucklebow and two arms, was in use. This was the probable forerunner of a weapon that was to remain popular for the next century or so—the small-sword. By the last quarter of the seventeenth century the small-sword had acquired its basic form with a blade of around thirty inches in length, two small flat shells, a knucklebow, rear quillon often curved horizontally and an ovoid or urn-shaped pommel. Earlier specimens retain a simple, rather attenuated forward quillon. Two arms of the hilt spring from the quillon block and curve to meet the shells.

Delicate hilts of chiselled steel, gold, silver and brass were made and were sometimes further embellished with enamel plaques.

Styles naturally changed during its century or so of use, but one useful general guide in dating is the size of the arms of the hilt, for these tend to become smaller as the eighteenth century progresses. During the first few decades they are large enough to be of practical use, but by about 1760–1765 they have become so reduced as to be no more than decorative. Shells are a further guide to dating, as on early small-swords they were of equal size, but as the period progressed the inner shell was reduced in size. Finally the late swords have a single disc guard whilst military swords acquired a single boat-shape guard.

Blades in a variety of shapes were produced, but they may be divided into three main groups—the ordinary flat, oval section blade, the hollow ground triangular section blade, and finally the *colichemarde*. This latter type is immediately recognisable by its thick top, or forte, of the blade which narrows sharply at a point roughly a third of the length of the blade, to a very much thinner section, tapering off to the point. Designed to give strength at the top for parrying an opponent's blade, it still allowed easy, quick use of the point.

Small-swords were worn supported on two chains of differing lengths suspended from a steel hook which was slipped over a belt or waist band. Two spring clips engaged with the rings attached to metal bands on the scabbard which was usually of leather or parchment-covered wood.

Another weapon, very typical of the seventeenth and eighteenth centuries, was the hanger or hunting sword, for both terms are very often applied indiscriminately to the same weapon. These weapons are usually short and light with a blade of around twenty inches in length, fitted to a very simple hilt comprising a single knucklebow, short down-curving rear quillon and a high percentage have a small shell, or scallop, projecting from one side of the quillons. The metal parts of the hilt may be of brass, silver or steel and are frequently decorated with mythological or hunting motifs. Grips

are of staghorn, wood or veneered with horn or tortoiseshell. Blades are almost invariably single edged but may be curved or straight—as a working generalisation it may be said that the later ones are far more often straight. Similarly, brass-hilted hangers were primarily military weapons.

Another type of sword which flourished during this same period was the basket-hilted sword, although its early history is not at all clear. Germany was the probable country of origin and the earliest recorded forms appear around the middle of the sixteenth century. A great majority of styles are described as basket hilts, but their common feature is a cage of bars which cover the hand when holding the hilt. This cage may be formed by a few fairly wide bars or else by a complex interweaving of narrower metal strips. During the English Civil Wars of 1642–1648 both Royalists and Roundheads favoured a cavalry sword with a straight blade and a fairly simple metal basket.

Increased mechanisation during the eighteenth century hastened a process which had started much earlier: that is, the growing emphasis on standardisation of military equipment. During the seventeenth and eighteenth centuries commanding officers had almost complete discretion in the manner of arming their units, but this freedom was gradually diminished and regulations were issued setting out details of the appropriate swords. In fact, many officers placed varying constructions on the regulations so that absolute standardisation was not to be obtained for some time. British infantrymen carried a sword until 1786, when they were officially withdrawn. Officers, of course, continued to carry swords and most of these were in the general style of a small-sword with a fairly light blade. In 1796 an order was made setting out details of these swords: a hilt of gilt brass with a straight blade, although this might be single or double edged. Heavy cavalry swords were also defined as being straight bladed, unlike those of the light cavalry who used a broad-bladed sabre with a simple stirrup hilt. It was at this same period that the steel scabbard first appeared in general use in Britain. In 1822 another innovation appeared in the form of the so-called Gothic hilt, which is a simple half basket, and it is this style which has survived to the present.

Swords were carried by most naval officers and differed considerably according to the occasion. The Royal Navy, indeed all navies, indulged in considerable ceremony and for these occasions a light, dress small-sword was popular, but for combat a heavy, often curved weapon was preferred and in all cases the officer was free to indulge his own taste. Official regulation patterns appear to have been established around 1801 but it was not until 1825 that full details were recorded. Three types were specified for the various ranks and two years later in 1827 a new pattern was defined and this had the half basket hilt which is still used today. Blades and hilt details have been varied over the years and particulars of these may be found in the appropriate reference books.

For seamen in a boarding party a cutlass of simple rugged construction was normal issue. Cheap and lacking all trimming, these swords were used in conjunction with boarding axes and short boarding pikes.

Although the sword was discarded by the British infantry in the middle of the eighteenth century, troops still carried their bayonets and this edged weapon still survives today. The name bayonet derives from the town of Bayonne in the extreme southwest of France, although originally the word was applied only to a type of knife.

Bayonets of the seventeenth century were of the type known as plug bayonets since they were simply pushed into the musket barrel. They had a plain, turned wooden grip which, apart from a bulbous swelling near the quillons, tapered slightly to fit firmly into the barrel. Quillons, often of brass, were quite short and the broad, double-edged blade tapered gradually to the point. Although this form of bayonet was discarded in most of Europe by the beginning of the seventeenth century, it persisted in Spain for

another hundred years. Plug bayonets converted the empty musket into a short pike, but once in position it meant that the musket could not be loaded and military designers sought means to overcome this serious drawback. The first step was to affix rings to the hilt and these slipped over the barrel so securing the bayonet yet leaving the barrel free for loading and firing. By the end of the seventeenth century the French had evolved a far more efficient system whereby the blade was fitted to a short tube which slipped over the barrel and was held in place by engaging with a lug on the barrel. Socket bayonets like these were to remain in general use until around the middle of the nineteenth century.

Socket bayonets had long, stiff, narrow, tapering blades, which limited their use to that of a thrusting weapon. Attempts were soon being made to produce a bayonet which could also be used as a sword, and in Britain one of the first of such weapons was the brass-hilted bayonet for the Baker rifle, issued to certain regiments of the army around 1800.

Around the middle of the nineteenth century there was an increasing change from the socket fixing to that used on such weapons as the Baker bayonet. A slit was cut into the grip and this engaged with a lug on the barrel and when the bayonet was pushed into position a spring-clip locked it firmly into place. This system is still in use on most of the military weapons today.

Unlike the bayonet the dagger has really never been a predominantly military weapon although it is, of course, historically much older with its beginnings in the flint handaxes of the Stone Age. By definition a dagger is essentially a weapon with a tapering double-edged blade, whilst a knife has, again by definition, only one sharpened edge, but in fact it is often not easy to be precise when describing certain specimens. As a military weapon a dagger does not appear until the middle of the thirteenth century, but obviously most soldiers had carried some kind of small edged weapon from earliest times. Changes in style were fewer than with swords and at any given period several types might well be in use. Thus a soldier of the fourteenth century might have carried any one of perhaps four common types. There are many contemporary references to a dagger called an anlace, but its precise appearance is uncertain although it seems likely that it had a long thin blade and was essentially a thrusting weapon. A baselard, also in use at this period, was a larger weapon with a larger, wider blade and a simple hilt shaped like a capital I. Civilians as well as soldiers often carried a ballock or kidney dagger which had a hilt fashioned entirely from wood and whose guard was formed by two small lobes projecting from either side of the grip. The simplicity of design and construction ensured a long life for this type of dagger and it was in general use until the seventeenth century.

At this particular time, some schools of fencing emphasised the use of a dagger to parry an opponent's blade and these left-hand daggers were commonly made in a variety of styles. Some are distinguished only by a ring on one side of the quillons whilst a few are fitted with blades serrated on one edge to entangle an opponent's blade.

During the seventeenth and early eighteenth centuries it was common practice for artillery men to carry a dagger which was adapted for use as a measuring and calculating device. Gunner's stilettoes almost invariably had long, stiff, triangular blades and one of the blade faces was engraved with a series of lines and numbers. By measuring the bore or inside diameter of the gun barrel with the blade the gunner could then read off the correct weight of shot required. A variety of scales were used and a few blades will be found with three sets to give readings for lead, iron, or stone shot. Grips are frequently of wood, but many are all steel.

As the seventeenth century progressed a number of changes took place in the British way of life—greater use of cutlery, more settled times, a growing military emphasis on firearms—and all these factors tended to make the carrying of daggers unnecessary. Clasp knives were introduced and these served all general needs except in such places as the American colonies where daggers and knives were carried by large numbers of people until well into the present century. Of these edged weapons probably none is better known than the bowie knife, although in fact the exact definition of a bowie knife is very much in dispute. It was named after a man who led a colourful and romantic life, full of high adventure, duels and legendary exploits before he finally met his death fighting for a lost cause at the Alamo in Texas in 1836. James Bowie's original knife is usually accepted as being heavy and long bladed with a clipped point and a sharpened false edge. A very short time after Bowie's death all kinds of weapons were being described as bowies, including many that were merely sheath knives, and this habit has continued to the present.

Cutlers from Sheffield were quick to realise the potential market for such weapons and soon were producing them in bulk. George Wostenholm was the first to appreciate the possibilities and his knives were of good quality and bore his trademark IXL, but this was soon copied by his competitors. With an eye to the U.S. market the cutlers had appropriate patriotic mottoes and exhortations etched on the blades, including many that suggest they were made in the United States. The size of these knives varied greatly as did the style of blade and hilt, whilst most had tooled leather sheaths with metal lockets and chapes. Some bowies were manufactured in India, but these are distinguished by guards which are wider and far more elliptical than those on English and American weapons, which are usually straight and fairly narrow.

After the American Civil War of 1861 to 1865, bowie production decreased and fighting knives lost much of their popularity, and it was not until the development of trench warfare during the First World War that knives were again seriously considered as weapons.

An English sword with a finely engraved mortuary type hilt. The 42¾-inch blade is sixteenth century and the hilt seventeenth century.

W. Howarth.

An English 'hanger' or hunting sword in a style usually called 'Hounslow'. It has a 24½-inch blade. Made about 1650.

W. Howarth.

143

A mid-seventeenth-century cavalry sword. It has a bone fluted grip which is a later replacement.

A. V. Smith.

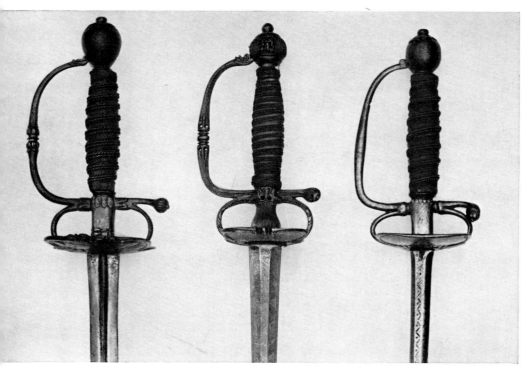

Three examples of seventeenth-century small-side rapiers.

A. Wade.

An early eighteenth-century sword used by dragoons. Note the lion's head on the top of the pommel.

G. Mungeam.

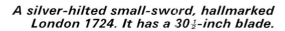
A silver-hilted small-sword, hallmarked London 1724. It has a 30½-inch blade.

An officer's sword or 'spadroon'. Blade 32 inches and made c. 1780.

A. Miller.

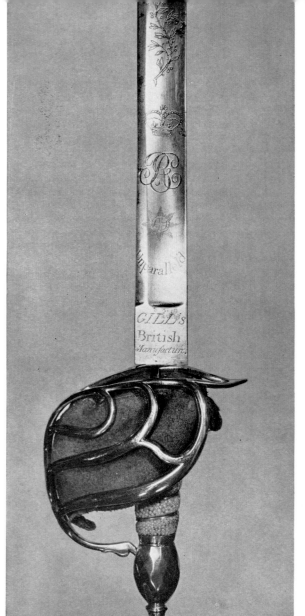

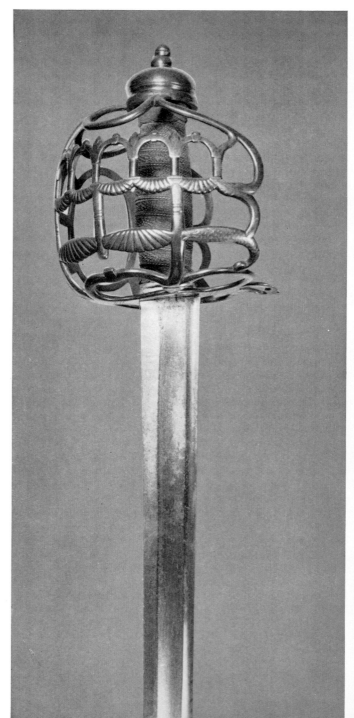

A fine example of a heavy cavalry sword made by Thomas Gill of Birmingham, 1788. The guard is of brass and the pommel is steel.
W. Howarth.

An English cavalry sword of about 1775. Note the fine quality basket engraved with fishes and serpents and a wirebound sharkskin grip.
W. Howarth.

Left: *Light Cavalry sabre of the 1796 pattern and made by John Gill.*
Right: *a similar pattern made by Woolley & Co. of Birmingham.*
Below left: *a fine pistol-sword of mid-eighteenth century.*
Below: *Infantry Officer's sword of about 1810.*

L. Archer and A. Miller.

Here am I, little jumping Joan,
When nobody's with me,
I'm always alone.

An illustration from Kate Greenaway's (1846–1901) Mother Goose. Two features of her work which still attracts people are her delightfully innocent children and the well observed contemporary costumes in which she dressed them.

One of the illustrations by Sir John Tenniel to Alice in Wonderland, published in 1865 and engraved by the Dalziel Brothers.

One of the original illustrations to Charles Dickens' Pickwick Papers by Phiz, otherwise H. R. Browns (1815–82).

BOOKS, PRINTS AND MAPS

There is no artificiality in dealing with books, prints and maps in the same chapter, for they have much in common. In all three cases a mechanical or semi-mechanical process has been used to produce a work of art (in its widest sense) in a number of identical versions. In addition, the three subjects are in many cases intermingled; a book may be illustrated with printed illustrations or maps; and maps or prints, without text, may be bound together in book form. Indeed it is unfortunate that many of these books have lost their composite form: the prints and maps have often been detached from their bindings and sold separately, while they were originally designed to complement each other, each to tell one something about the other. Separated, the books may become dull and the prints are more easily damaged.

Whether one is interested in antiques because one regards them as sound investments or for aesthetic reasons, book collecting still offers a very rich field. The most important book is so easily concealed under a dowdy exterior that it may lie hidden for years, and so it is likely that the second-hand bookshops and auctioneers will have a good supply for many years to come. Of course, one is no longer likely to come across an undiscovered Caxton or any other *incunabulum*—one of the very small number of books that were printed in England before 1500. Yet persistence and regular visits to bookshops still lead to remarkable finds.

In such a very wide field, it is important to specialise to some extent. To buy books merely because they are old and rare is nonsense. Scarceness adds nothing to the quality of a book—indeed, some books were made artificially scarce by means of issuing them in limited editions—but may make it undeservedly expensive. In addition, a collection of books selected for their scarcity may be dull; a collection based on a particular taste of the collector is unlikely to be so.

Many people collect books from all periods on a special subject that interests them, or first editions of the work of a favourite author. Others look to the illustrations, and here there is tremendous scope. The first illustrated book printed in England—*The Mirror of the World*—came from Caxton's press in 1481, but illustrated books have continued to be produced in every generation since then. Illustrated books of the eighteenth century can still be found easily, and the nineteenth century saw the production of many books that took advantage of technical innovations and contained beautifully printed illustrations of well-known artists. The illustrations to the stories of Dickens by Phiz are known to everyone, as are John Tenniel's drawings for *Alice in Wonderland*, engraved by the Dalziel Brothers. Another famous partnership between artist and engraver was that of Kate Greenaway, creator of whimsical designs full of long-frocked children, and the engraver who so carefully printed them in colour, Edmund Evans. But, apart from the work of Greenaway and the other children's designers—George Cruikshank, Richard Doyle,

Beatrix Potter—there is reflected in nine-teenth-century books all the various streams of Victorian art: the sentimental poses of Arthur Hughes, the luminous, delicate colours of Birkett Foster's country scenes, the simple, harsh reality of Gustav Doré, and the birth of Art Nouveau in the work of Walter Crane.

Many collectors are principally interested in the exterior decoration of books. One of its most delightful forms is fore-edge printing, in which the leaves of a book are slightly fanned out by turning back the front cover and are then decorated in water-colour. Later, the edges are gilded in the usual manner so that the painting is concealed except when the book is open. The earliest dated example in a Bible of 1651, with a fore-edge painting of armorials, but most of this work is eighteenth and nineteenth century. William Edwards of Halifax introduced the idea of painting landscapes and portraits in the mid eighteenth century and he may also have pioneered the double-paintings—in which one scene appeared when the leaves were fanned to the left, another when they were fanned to the right —which appeared from about 1788 onwards.

Styles of bookbinding have been constantly changing since books were first produced, as have the materials used. Sheep or deerskin was the most common material until the fifteenth century, but it gradually declined in the estimation of the rich until it was used only on the cheapest work in the eighteenth century. For the binding of fine books it was replaced by calf and limp vellum in the sixteenth century, morocco and vellum in the seventeenth century, calf and morocco in the eighteenth century. In the nineteenth century all these materials were largely ousted by bookcloth, which has remained the standard covering for the boards to the present day.

The chief processes of decoration used on the binding have been tooling and blocking. In the former, decoration and lettering is impressed by hand on the covers of books by means of brass letters, dies, pallets and rolls.

It may be either tooled in blind—that is, without further decoration—or have an additional decoration of gold leaf. Books with bindings tooled in blind have probably been made in England since the seventh century, if the Stoyhurst Gospel is a good example. The earliest known gilt binding was bound, probably for Cardinal Wolsey, in 1519. Books could be decorated on a larger scale by means of blocking, for which bigger dies and a press were employed. Here too, the blocking could be blind, or incorporate with foil or gold leaf.

There have been many ephemeral styles of binding in addition to the established ones we have already mentioned. In Elizabethan England, for example, the decoration of velvet covered boards with embroidery in gold and silver thread was very popular. Styles of blocking and tooling changed continuously. The Victorians revelled in every available kind of decorative technique and combined quite different techniques with one another. Thus a binding might be of green cloth, blocked in gold and black with with orange paper inlays. The twentieth century has seen little fine decorative binding, but a notable exception was the work of the binders at the Gregynog Press, who between 1913 and 1945 produced very high quality binding in a modern style.

The Gregynog Press was a private press, that is, it produced small editions of carefully printed and illustrated books of its own choice. Such books are an excellent subject for the collector, for the private presses that were successful produced some of the most interesting and original works of their times. Horace Walpole, for example, printed books in the eighteenth century Gothic house, Strawberry Hill, which he built at Twickenham. Thomas Johnes, whose interests ranged as widely as Walpole's, taking in landscape gardening, improving agriculture, and a magnificent collection of pictures and books stored in his home at Hafod in Wales, also printed books there between 1803 and 1810, notably the *Chronicles* of Froissart. And, towards the end of the nineteenth century,

One of the wood-
cuts in John
Caxton's Golden
Legend, published
c. 1483.

Left: *a fine example of deep blocking in several colours and typical of nineteenth century cover
design.*
Right: *a page from the 'Kelmscott' Chaucer published in 1896. The woodcuts are after original
drawings by Sir Edward Burne-Jones. This work was the highlight of William Morris's famous
Kelmscott Press.*

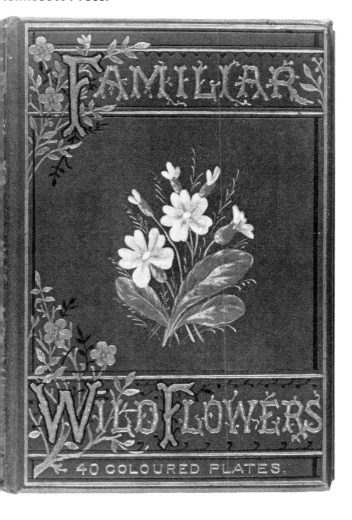

William Morris, who had already repudiated contemporary attitudes towards architecture, fabric and furniture design, and politics, also took a completely new look at bookmaking. At his Kelmscott Press, he made his own paper, cut his own types, and together with his friend Burne-Jones, set about the separate designing of each double page as a work of art. Though the twentieth century has rejected the idea of a return to medievalism, typography and book design have become lively and respected arts, due in no small measure to the work of Morris.

Prints

The earliest prints, as well as many modern prints, are from woodcuts. They were frequently used in late medieval books. Their place was taken by line engraving on copper towards the end of the sixteenth century, and it was only with the coming of Thomas Bewick (1753–1828) that the use of wood was revived. His wood engravings of birds and animals for such books as Aesop's *Fables* have never been matched since in their delicacy and integrity of design. Wood engravings remained popular until the end of the nineteenth century and were used by most of the well-known Victorians—the Pre-Raphaelites, the painters of conventional Victorian subjects, and the wealth of talented illustrators who contributed to *Punch* and similar magazines. Wood engravings were also used in the process patented by George Baxter in 1835 for making coloured prints by means of successive printings from differently coloured blocks.

While the wood engraver cut away the wood to leave ridges which held the ink, the metal engraver used the intaglio method. Using a 'burin', he cut lines in a copper plate; when ink was passed over the plate it would collect in these lines, and their image could then be transferred to the paper. The first important native-born engraver was William Rogers, who worked late in the sixteenth century. His seventeenth century successors engraved mainly portraits, and their prints were generally interpretations of

the work of contemporary portrait painters. The art of fine engraving declined after the passing of William Faithorne (1616–1691) and Francis Barlow (1626–1702), but painters found that engraved versions of their pictures could greatly increase their income. Thus William Hogarth (1697–1764) engraved versions of his social satires that were deliberately coarsened on the copper-plate to give them greater popular appeal. A more conscientious engraver was William Woollett (1735–1785), who made prints after George Stubbs, the sporting artist, and Richard Wilson. But the most powerful engravings of all time are from the hand of William Blake (1757–1827), artist, engraver, and one of the great intellects of his age, who translated the harsh visions of his imagination into formalised designs through the medium of the copperplate. The quality of engravings on metal rapidly declined after Blake, for the introduction of steel engraving, though it enabled many more prints to be produced from the one—later, also, because of the hardness of the metal, made for greater rigidity of design.

Early in the seventeenth century, a Czech, Wenceslaus Hollar (1607–1677) introduced the English to the art of etching, in which the lines are cut in the copperplate by means of acid. The plate is coated with a waxy substance and the drawing cut in the wax by means of an etching needle. When the plate is immersed in a bath of acid, the acid bites into the copper where the wax has been removed. This is known as hard ground etching. Two slightly different varieties of the same technique are chalk engraving, used to produce facsimiles of chalk drawings, and soft ground etching, which was introduced towards the end of the eighteenth century and made it possible to reproduce the texture of pencil or crayon drawing. Hollar produced a vast number of plates—over two thousand—embracing townscapes, costume, portraits and classical subjects. His friend Francis Place (1647–1728) etched many topographic subjects.

A further development of the art of the

A stipple engraving by G. Bartolozzi after Cipriani, published 1786. Bartolozzi was one of the most prolific printmakers of the eighteenth century, especially portraits and classical subjects.

St. Catherines's Hill near Guilford by J. M. W. Turner and published by him in 1811. This was one from Turner's magnificent and ambitious Liber Studorium.

During recent years fashion prints of the nineteenth century have been much sought after. They not only capture completely the spirit of Victorian times but are also fine examples of graphic art. Many were drawn by French artists for English consumption. The one shown here was originally reproduced in The Englishwoman's Domestic Magazine. This was the popular journal whose fashion editor for many years was Mrs. Beeton, better known for her work on household management.

153

Two-tone lithograph by T. Picken of Thirlemere and Wytheburn after a drawing by J. B. Pyne, published June 1859.

Monochrome lithograph by J. Laporte of a Study of Trees after a drawing by T. Gainsborough, published Sept. 1803.

Engraving by W. Byrne of the Priory Church at Haddington after a drawing by Thomas Hearne, published March 1786.

etcher produced what is probably the chief illustrative technique of the later eighteenth century—the aquatint. This made it possible to produce from a copperplate a print that had a tone very similar to that of a watercolour. The tone, which was produced by covering the surface of the plate with minute ink-cells (by means of a special ground) etched to varying depths, was usually combined with etched or dry-point lines. After printing, the paper could be coloured by hand. Paul Sandby is the first great name associated with aquatinting, but, following his lead, all kinds of artists began to make use of the medium. There were the topographical aquatints of William and Thomas Daniell, the boxing, racing and hunting scenes, the prints of the great sporting paintings of H. T. Alken (1785–1851), many of which he engraved himself, the coaching scenes and the patriotic prints produced during the French Wars. There are many outstanding prints from this period, and none more so than the satires, cartoons and caricatures of Joseph Gillray (1757–1815) and Thomas Rowlandson (1750–1827). Charles Turner also did some fine work, including his twenty-four aquatints after J. M. W. Turner's *Liber Studorum*.

The mezzotint was the most arduous print to produce, but was also a very successful method of reproduction in that, like the aquatint, it consisted of tones rather than lines. The surface of the plate was pitted all over by means of a tool known as a 'rocker'. This left the plate covered with burrs which held ink and printed black if left untouched. But the engraver could produce intermediate tones or pure white, as well as black, by partially or wholly scraping away the burrs. Prince Rupert introduced the process into England in the late seventeenth century, and it was soon seen what an excellent technique it was for reproducing paintings in monochrome. John Raphael Smith (1752–1812) is the greatest name among the portrait mezzotinters and he made many plates after Reynolds and Romney. David Lucas (1802–1881) made superb translations on to the copperplate of the landscapes of Constable with an amazing truth to the originals.

Lithography came to England at the beginning of the nineteenth century and immediately attracted artists because of its directness, which enabled the work of their hands to be reproduced without the necessity of learning arduous and difficult processes. The artist draws with a greasy crayon on a flat stone and then sponges the surface with an acid to fix the drawing. Next, he moistens the whole with water which is only absorbed by the stone where it is not greasy. When greasy ink is passed over the stone, the water again rejects it, but it adheres to the drawing and can thus be printed. The early prints were often hand-coloured, but in the 1840s they began to be printed in colours by using a separate stone for each colour. Two superb publications are especially worth a mention from this early period: R. P. Bonington's *Voyages pittoresques et romantiques dans l'ancienne France* and T. S. Boy's *Picturesque Architecture in Paris, Ghent, Antwerp, Rouen* (1839). The lithograph was rather degraded by late Victorian artists, but has again become a respected medium in our own day.

Maps

Maps have been reproduced by most of the processes used for prints, except those that required tone—copperplate engraving, etching, woodcutting and lithography. The first two processes can be easily recognised as they leave a 'plate-mark'—a shallow depression over the area of the plate caused by the round edges of the block when it is impressed on the paper.

The map that interests the collector is a very different affair from the maps of today. Commonplace information was embellished with decorative details and the borders were used to give information that was not strictly cartographical at all. The title of the map and the imprint were commonly enclosed in a decorative cartouche incorporating scrollwork, figures, architectural designs or local scenes. Free spaces round the border of the

John Speed's map of Hertford-shire from his *Atlas of Great Britain,* published 1611.

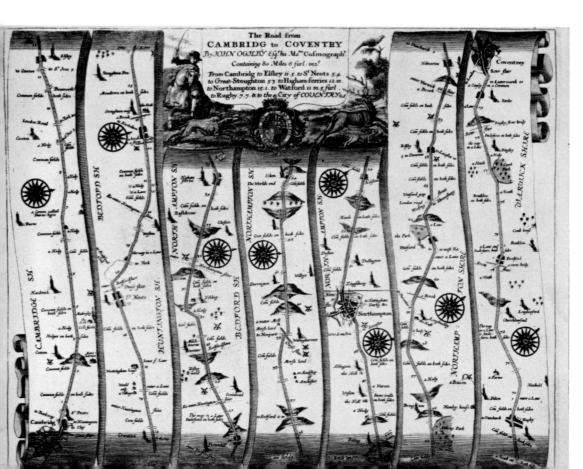

John Ogilby's map of the road from Cambridge to Coventry. One of a series of one hundred of the first road maps to cover the main post roads of England and Wales.

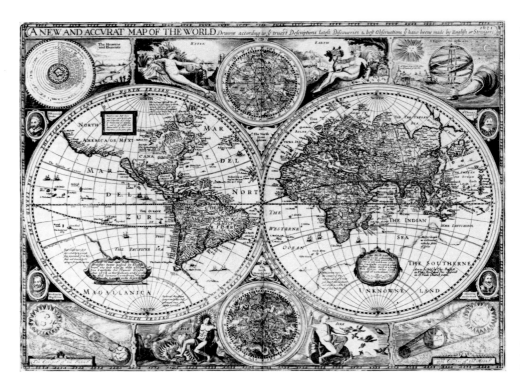

John Speed's map of the world, published in 1676.

All maps reproduced by courtesy of Baynton-Williams.

map would often be filled up by small informative insets of town plans, noteworthy local buildings, or the coats of arms of the local families, while spaces in the body of the map where there was little detailed information to be given gave the engraver an opportunity to add pictorial detail such as wild animals, sea beasts, ships and people in local costume. Even such commonplace details as the scale and compass were presented decoratively; the compass commonly in the form of a rose, the scale embellished with surveyor's instruments. There is often great variety in the lettering and many maps were coloured by the map sellers before being put on sale.

Only a few of the better known mapmakers can be mentioned here. It is worth noting in passing that many plates outlived those who originally engraved and published them. They were handed down and passed from publisher to publisher, new information being added and the imprint changed with each change of ownership. It can be an interesting study for the map-collector to watch the process of a plate through successive editions.

The earliest important maps to be printed in England from the copperplate were those of Christopher Saxton, whose county maps were published between 1574 and 1579. Under a mandate from the Queen, he conducted the first proper survey of England and Wales, county by county. He did not engrave his own plates—few cartographers did—but employed Augustine Ryther, a Yorkshireman, on some and Flemish refugees on others.

John Speed (1552–1629) issued his *Theatre of the Empire of Great Britain* in 1611. It was a commercial venture and a very successful one, for the plates continued to be used until the late eighteenth century. Though Speed supplied the materials for these maps—which he obtained from many and varied sources—their quality is due to the work of the great Amsterdam engraver Jodocus Hondius.

John Ogilby (1600–1676), produced road maps in a new and interesting form by depicting them in long strips, with details of houses, inns and the countryside along the way. At the end of the eighteenth century there is the important work of Aaron and John Arrowsmith.

157

A York 'Acorn' flagon, a form exclusive to York and Wigan pewterers. Specimens are found without a spout. Note the typical 'Yorkshire' spout. Height 9 inches.
Art Gallery of
New South Wales.

PEWTER

Pewter is an alloy whose essential ingredient is tin. It was made by the Romans, some of it, perhaps, in England, for the raw materials of the trade—tin and lead—were readily available. The history of English pewter is the history of its struggle with other materials, greater and lesser. In the early middle ages, it was regarded as a respectable alternative to the rarer metals. An ecclesiastical synod of Rouen in 1074 permitted chalices to be made of pewter in default of gold and silver. By the thirteenth century though, the chalices that were now used at Mass had to be gold and silver, pewter chalices were made to be buried with the priest. By the end of the middle ages however, the market for pewter was expanding rapidly as society was transformed. Men were breaking out of the strict gradations of the social structure that was based on the landlord–tenant relationship, and the 'new-rich'—the yeoman, farmer and urban shop-keeper—were willing to spend money on household utensils worthy of their status. Treen was for the poor; they would have pewter. At the same time, new techniques were being mastered in England. The seventeenth century saw the first indigenous production of table-glass in England, and pottery was becoming an industry. By the next century glass was being made for ordinary people and so was china. Now it was pewter that became vulgar though it was not finally ousted until the Victorians learnt that it was not respectable not to have silver in one's canteen and under one's candles,

and china and cut glass on one's table.

The composition of pewter became standardised at an early date. During the reign of Edward III the London pewterers petitioned the Mayor and Aldermen of the City of London for legislation designed to protect their trade from 'unfair competition' (i.e. to make the trade a closed shop), and to assure the good quality of English pewter. The result of their persuasions was the Ordinances of the Pewterers of 1348. It was provided, among other things, that all flat-ware (plates and dishes) were to be of 'fine' pewter, that is 'with the proportion of copper to the tin, as much as of its own nature will take'. All other objects wrought in pewter by the trade (for instance, cruets and candlesticks) were to have a composition of 26 pounds of lead to each hundredweight of tin; a very similar substance later became known as 'lazy' metal. Though not mentioned in the Ordinances, an even poorer quality of metal was generally used where loss of shape was not important and a fine appearance was not needed, as in the case of commercial objects and toys.

In 1473, the industry was well established, for in that year it was granted its first charter and took its place among the City Livery Companies. Its power to control and standardise the production of pewter was extended by the grant of the right of search which enabled members to seek out false wares, forfeit them and fine their makers. This right was pursued with enthusiasm by the London pewterers until the seventeenth

A relief decorated beaker. The top band bears the wording TO DRINK AND BE MERRYE IS NOT AMISS—AND WITH THY FRED (FRIEND) ABIDE—THE MIRTH AND DRINKING TAKE HEED THOU DOEST NOT (CHIDE), R.B. *Early seventeenth century. Height 6 inches.*

London Museum.

century, when the country pewterers began to resent their authority. Consequently, the right of search fell into disuse outside London, with the unfortunate result that country pewter, and the general reputation of English pewter abroad, began to decline.

A further enactment of 1503 also helped to maintain standards. This made it compulsory for makers to put their marks, known as 'touches', on their products. It became the custom—no one knows exactly

when—for the maker to stamp the impression of his mark on a panel of metal, a 'touch plate', which was kept in the Pewterers' Hall in Lime Street. The Hall and its contents were destroyed in the Great Fire in 1666, but a new building had been put up by the end of the next year, and the touches of existing pewterers were taken again. There is now a complete record, therefore, of all London pewter makers going right back to those who began work in the 1640s.

Pewter marks were primarily used to identify the maker. They were not intended, like silver marks, to date the piece. The date of a piece of pewter can only be guessed at by examining the style and discovering when the maker registered his touch and when he died.

Marks were also used to register good or bad quality. In 1474, base pewter was disfigured with a 'broad arrowhead', later to be forfeited and destroyed. A good quality piece of pewter might be officially stamped, in 1509, with the 'lily pot' and the 'strake', both of which appear in the Companies' arms, or with the fleur-de-lys in 1548. The Rose and Crown was variously used, sometimes as a mark of quality, often without official approval, sometimes to show that the goods were intended to be exported. The crowned letter 'X' had a very chequered career, although it was originally used to denote hard metal.

In addition to the maker's touch and the marks mentioned above there are often four small marks, very like silver hallmarks in appearance, on pewter. These usually contain the initials or the name of the maker. If they contain a date, it will be the date of registration of the touch, not the date of manufacture. In some cases they contain the initials of more than one maker, and it has been suggested that this signifies some kind of trade arrangement between makers, by which one maker made pieces of a certain type for another maker to sell, either because some makers preferred to specialise or because they lacked the ability or the equipment to make certain pieces.

A great deal of pewter is not decorated at

An early English spoon with 'fig-shaped' bowl and believed to be thirteenth century.
Worshipful Company of Pewterers.

all. It is a material eminently suited to show off the virtues of fine, simple designs and throughout most of its career it was modelled in pleasing, functional shapes. Yet there was also some fine decorative work done in pewter, especially in the seventeenth century.

A style of decoration was dictated to a large extent by the nature of the metal. It was too soft to be line-engraved really successfully, and a completed engraving was easily worn smooth. In any case, the closed shop prevented not only manufacture, but also decoration, of pewter by outsiders so that artists were excluded from the work. Yet there are good examples extant of one kind of engraving, known as 'wriggled-work'. For this, the engraver used a gouge-like tool with a sharp, narrow blade, which he held at an angle and pushed across the metal, rocking the blade from side to side all the time.

A rarer kind of decoration was achieved by means of a punch cut with an ornamental design in relief which was transferred to the pewter, like the touches, by resting it on the pewter and giving the reverse end a blow from a hammer. Continuous ornament could thus be built up around the border of a plate, composed of crescents, roses, fleur-de-lys or other conventional designs.

The commonest method of decorating hollow-ware was to make a pattern on the inside of the mould used to cast the piece. The object would thus be made and given cast decoration in a single process. The William Grainger candlestick in the Victoria and Albert Museum is probably the most celebrated example of this technique.

The range of pewter produced was very great and it is difficult to categorise it satisfactorily. The division into flat-ware and hollow-ware covers many of the better-known kinds of pewter—plates, chargers and porringers coming under the former and drinking vessels, measures, candlesticks and cruets under the latter—but this does leave out things like spoons. However, this simple division, with the addition of one or two extra-curricular items, is probably the best for a short general survey.

Flat ware, also commonly known as sad-ware, was beaten by the maker to ensure maximum strength, and this rule, together with the regulations about composition, were strictly enforced by the Pewterers' Company. At the least the goods would be confiscated and a fine levied, but if a pewterer persisted in breaking the rules he risked imprisonment or expulsion from the Company. Fine pewter had always to be used for the group of closely related items that commonly appeared on the table—plates, dishes, chargers, platters and trenchers. Dating these pieces is difficult, especially if they were made before the seventeenth century. In the early seventeenth century pewterers were making broad-rimmed dishes with no decoration on the rim, and they continued to do so until the third quarter of the century, though the width of the rim gradually decreased. From about 1675 the rim began to be decorated, at first with multiple reeding gouged out on a lathe, later with reeding cast on to the surface as part of the process of making the dish. Cast moulding continued to be standard during the first half of the eighteenth century, though the reeding was usually single. In the last period of pewter manufacture the reeding

disappeared altogether, though the moulding on the underside of the plate rim was thickened.

The Ordinances included porringers among those vessels which were required to be made of 'fine' metal. These were small, shallow vessels, with a flat, horizontal handle or handles, and they were used for liquid or semi-liquid foods. In the mid-sixteenth century they were made with two ears cast in the form of a fleurs-de-lys, while from the beginning of the seventeenth century onwards it was established practice to have one ear only. The early blood porringers or

An early chalice with 'ogee' bowl, single-knopped stem and bell-shaped foot. Dated first quarter of the seventeenth century. Height 7 inches.
Victoria & Albert Museum.

bleeding bowls are probably not distinguishable from their contemporary porringers, indeed the two may have been to a large extent interchangeable throughout their history in spite of the fact that one was used for food and the other for blood letting. Some bleeding bowls, however, have lines inside to mark liquid capacity. Smaller bowls, on the same pattern as these, are probably wine-tasters.

Larger, two-handled cups have to be classified according to the purpose for which they were made, and this is not always clear. There are the 'caudle cups', used to give spiced wine drinks, usually for a medicinal purpose, and the Posset pots, which cannot be clearly distinguished from each other, though posset—a drink with a base of ale or sack combined with cream, sugar and nut-meg—is quite different from caudle. Toasting cups were larger again, as they were made to be handed round the table and supply the whole company with drink. The wassail bowl was generally used for mixing the drinks at table. Both are related to the smaller loving cup, which, at least in its later days, was intended to be a memento, and was engraved for presentation at weddings. Incidentally, few footed loving cups were made before the middle of the eighteenth century.

The pre-Reformation Church in England did not use pewter for the highest offices after the twelfth century, as we have already said, but it continued to be used to make pieces fit for burial with priests, as well as cruets. A great deal of church pewter has survived from all periods, for, though it had been rendered obsolete by silver, it was carefully preserved in the Churches until recent times when the new fashion for collecting pewter made it financially worth while to sell it all off. In particular, this meant that many of the fine pewter flagons have been preserved in excellent condition. The clergy had been instructed in 1603 to use a pot or stoup of pewter 'if not of purer metal' to bring the communion wine to the table, and this gave a fillip to the industry. The typical flagon made before 1675 had a body of a tapering cylindrical form, a plain curved handle and a moulded foot, which grew wider as the century progressed, and a bun shaped cover or in the case of the 'Beefeater' flagons, a lid shaped like the caps of the Yeomen Warders of the Tower. From the end of the seventeenth century the most common type was of a tall cylindrical shape topped with a domed cover surmounted with a finial. In defiance of the London fashions, some acorn-shaped flagons were produced in Yorkshire and are thus called 'York' flagons.

Pewter plates with flat rims and deep central wells, which many churches possessed until the early twentieth century, may have been patens proper—plates intended to hold the bread at communion—but were probably used latterly as flagon stands, if they had not been originally made for that purpose. Alms dishes, too were made of pewter and a few of them were elaborately decorated.

The drinking vessels and measures are probably the best known pieces of pewter, and are great favourites with collectors. Pewter drinking vessels have probably been made since the industry began, though early examples cannot be accurately dated. We know that 'tanggard potts' and 'stope potts' were being made in the fifteenth century, and many varieties of beakers, bowls and cups in the sixteenth century. The Stuart beakers were tall and slender enough to be elegant, but in the eighteenth century beakers tended to become squat and stumpy. The early tankards were probably not distinguishable from measures, but flat-topped tankards were being made in the last half of the seventeenth century. Domed covers appeared shortly before 1685, together with a new type of handle terminated by a 'ball' or, from 1710, by a 'fish-tail'. From about

Three fine seventeenth century candlesticks, those at left and right with octagonal base, drip tray and top flange; c. 1860–90. The centre specimen is of slightly later date, with a hollow knop in centre of the column.

Richard Mundey.

1730 onwards the tulip-shaped tankard became more typical, normally with a domed cover. Tapering, lidless tankards were also produced in considerable quantity in the eighteenth century.

The earliest identifiable measures are the Baluster Measures, which probably originated in the mid-sixteenth century, though measures had certainly been made in pewter long before that. But pewter may never have had the field to itself, for throughout the seventeenth century the pewterers complained about and petitioned against the use of earthenware measures. A committee of the House of Commons resolved in 1696 that only sealed measures made of pewter should be used in public houses, but it is clear that earthenware was never ousted. The baluster shape continued to be standard throughout the history of pewter, though some variety was achieved on lidded measures by varying the design of the thumb-piece. The bulbous spirit measures known as West country or 'Bristol' measures are of a quite different, jug-like shape.

We will now turn to candlesticks, salts and spoons. Pewter candlesticks were probably made from the earliest period until the metal was ousted by brass and silver in the 18th century. The 'Bell-based' style candlesticks were probably being made at the beginning of the seventeenth century. Octagonal bases largely disappeared during the reign of Queen Anne, when the drip-tray also became obsolete, giving way to the plain baluster form.

Everyone knows that peculiar significance was attached to salt until recent days and some sufficiently grand Master Salts were made, together with the smaller varieties which became popular from the seventeenth century onwards.

From the fourteenth century to the mid-seventeenth century, spoons had bowls that were broader at the base than they were next to the stem, that is the reverse of the present day spoon bowl. A spoon was often made distinctive by the knop which terminated the usually six-sided stem. It is the tremendous variety of these knops that attracts the collector: the 'ball' knops of the late fourteenth century; the 'horned headdress' knop of the fifteenth century; and the 'alderman', 'strawberry' and 'apostle' knops are among the many attractive types that may be discovered.

A flared beaker which can be dated 1610–12 since it bears a medallion of the three feathers of Bohemia and motto Ich Dien, flanked by 'H.B.', indicating Henry, Prince of Wales, son of James I. One of two known examples. Height 6 inches.

A group of plates of 8½ to 9¾ inches diameter, all with multiple-reeded rims. Dates range from 1675–90.

A pair of marriage plates with single-reeded rims. Both rim and base engraved in 'wriggled' work with lily-pots and initials. Made by James Hitchman, London. c. 1730. Diameter 8 inches.

An early period footed cup or chalice with bucket bowl on short hollow foot, the bowl inscribed with the date 1617.

Victoria & Albert Museum.

Broad-rimmed plate or paten with narrow cast reeding at edge and imitation hallmarks of the maker of c. 1650–60. Diameter 9¾ inches.

Sutherland Graeme Collection.

A porringer of Elizabeth I or earlier with the ears cast in one piece with the bowl. Bowl diameter 6½ inches.

Guildhall Museum.

Above: *two porringers with shallow straight-sided bowls. Left 5¼ inches and right 4½ inches diameter. Dated about 1650.*
Right: *porringer with flat 'fretted' ears with a crown and initials 'A.R.' (for Anne Regina) and made as a coronation souvenir in 1702. Made by Joseph King, London. Diameter 5 inches.*

Two early English baluster-shaped wine measures with 'ball and wedge' thumb-piece. They hold a quart and half pint, respectively. Seventeenth century.
Richard Mundey.

Two ale or cider jugs found in sizes ranging from one to three pints capacity ; c. 1790–1830.

H. W. L. Buckell.

Set of four West Country spirit measures, from the quart to the half-pint These were made in sizes ranging from three gallons to a half-gill, the largest having an additional handle beneath the spout to assist in carrying and pouring ; c. 1790–1830.

Two almost identical pairs of baluster candlesticks. One pair with the marks of George Lowes, Newcastle ; the others with the initials 'R.E.'. Date c. 1730.
C. A. Peel.

Three English flagons of the early and mid-eighteenth century.
Left: *with earlier form of handle, c. 1725–30.*
Centre: *with double-curved handle, c. 1750.*
Right: *with double curved handle, c. 1780. The two chalices at the front*
are c. 1740 (left) and c. 1760–70 (right). At rear are two 'alms' dishes, c. 1730.

Worshipful Company of Pewterers.

Three Georgian tavern mugs of pint capacity, c. 1735, c. 1780 and c. 1800 (left to
right). Note the change in the style of the handles.

173

A group of popular lidless, bulbous tavern measures made to Imperial
Measure and ranging from half-gallon to a miniature of one thirty-second
of a pint capacity. Mainly of c. 1826 and later.
Worshipful Company of Pewterers.

Left: *a William III flat-lid tankard with 'ramshorn' thumbpiece, c. 1695. Height 5½ inches.*
Centre: *a rare Charles II posset cup.*
Right: *a plain Stuart flat-lid tankard. Date c. 1680–90.*

Queen Anne 'loving' cup bearing the inscription GOD SAVE QUEEN ANNE and on the reverse the arms of the Worshipful Company of Pewterers. Height 6¾ inches.

Worshipful Company of Pewterers.

Above: *two examples of gilt brooches of characteristic Celtic design and dates from A.D. 740–50.*
Left: *an enamelled locket with jewelled lid which contained a miniature portrait of Queen Elizabeth I by Nicholas Hilliard. About the end of the sixteenth century.* **Below:** *an Anglo-Saxon silver ring engraved with zoomorphic figures. Ninth century.*
Waterton Collection.

JEWELLERY

With the exception of watercolours and prints, and, to a certain extent, books, the subject matter of this book does not include the 'fine' arts. The illustrations show pieces which are more or less functional as well as having aesthetic qualities. When we come to jewellery we are in a kind of half-way-house. At the beginning of the period of English jewellery, all the pieces are functional. Most of them are of religious significance—crosses, reliquaries and the like—and their decoration by craftsmen, like the building of a medieval cathedral, was part of the process of worship. Gradually, however, the balance between usefulness and beauty altered. Secular jewellery began to take pride of place. It was still functional, for most jewels were either an integral and vital part of the wearer's dress, or like the hat badges, indicated the wearer's politics. The secular designs characteristic of the Renaissance—the cupids, the scrolls, the classical subjects—replaced the conventional gothic designs and religious subjects. Jewellery became, momentarily, a vehicle for the great artists of the day such as Hans Holbein and attained a respected place among the fine arts. But this is only a brief period. Renaissance design, too, became conventional with the publication of engraved patterns for jewellers to copy. The designer and the maker were now different people—a division which William Morris saw as the chief cause of the decline in art. Jewellery itself became primarily a means of display. While talented men continued to produce good work

and new methods of cutting made it possible to display stones to greater advantage, jewels became superficial, in beauty and in purpose. The accent was on cut stones rather than on the settings so that there was no scope for the talents of great artists. It is possible to argue that the decline of fine jewellery began in the seventeenth century, 200 years before the decline of the other 'craftsmen' industries. Certainly by the eighteenth century it had ceased to be either functional or a 'fine' art.

The technical achievement and the sophistication of early jewellery is astonishing. The Sutton Hoo ship burial revealed items like clasps and purse mounts, probably produced by Anglo-Saxon craftsmen, decorated in complex and minute *cloisonné* work in garnets—an extremely difficult technique. As an example of late ninth century work we have the Alfred jewel (which, from its discovery in the Athelney Fens, and from the inscription 'AELFRED NEC HEHT GEWYRCAN'—'Alfred ordered me to be made'—is presumed to be connected with the famous king of Wessex). A half length figure with a flowered sceptre in each hand is depicted by means of *cloisonné* enamel in blue, green, brown and flesh tints. The case of the jewel is gold, part of it formed in the shape of a gaping boar's head.

In the eleventh and twelfth century, jewellery was the preserve of the goldsmith (and was to remain so for many years). The majority of goldsmiths worked in the security of workshops attached to great abbeys. Not till 1180 were the secular goldsmiths of London powerful and numerous enough to form themselves into a separate company. The style of clothing at that time gave little opportunity for the jeweller. The most characteristic secular jewel was the ring-brooch, which was held in place by the natural pull of the stuff through which the pin passed, not by a catch on the pin. These brooches were often inscribed with mottos such as 'IO SVI FLVR DE FIN AMVR' (I am a flower of perfect love), and such a brooch would clearly have been given as a love token. By the fourteenth century all kinds of ring-brooches were being produced; there were octagonal-shaped rings formed of six lobes and rings formed by two interlocking triangles. The style lasted much longer in Scotland than it did in most parts of England, though it is said to have remained as a part of traditional dress in Gloucestershire until the eighteenth century.

A change began to affect jewellery in the fourteenth century which was partly a matter of style and partly a result of the techniques and materials available. Jewellery reflected the contemporary fashions for natural beauty and manners. Precious stones were more easily available as the eastern trade of the powerful north Italian city-states expanded, and where stones had previously been in their natural cabochon shape, diamonds were now pointed and table-cut to give them brilliance. The art of translucent enamel in many different colours was developed and the goldsmiths developed new techniques, such as *pointille* engraving on gold. New demands were put on the jeweller by the more colourful and elegant clothing that appeared, but jewellery was not as widespread as its makers would have liked. In some powerful quarters it was still regarded as an important social symbol, not to be made easily available to people merely because they could afford to buy it. In 1363 the Statute de Victu et Vestitu decreed that handicraftsmen and yeomen, their wives and children were not to wear 'ceynture, cotel, fermaille, anel, garter, nouches, rubaignis,

cheines, bendes, seal u autre chose de ne dargent'.

Some jewellery of the fourteenth and fifteenth centuries had political significance. Brooches and badges carried heraldic designs and, at a later stage, were produced in lesser metals, such as lead gilt, and worn by the followers of great lords to show allegiance to a particular faction. A development of this were the collars of livery worn by royalty and the favourites of royalty, which later came to be the badges of distinguished orders and offices. Similar in form to the heraldic badges were the enseignes, the signs that pilgrims wore in their hats. These were made by casting in moulds and were sold at places of pilgrimage—gold and silver for the great, pewter and lead, sometimes gilded, for the poor.

Crowns were subject to fashion, like everything else, and had to be adapted to styles of hairdressing. In the fourteenth century for example, a crown often had to cover the jewelled *coiffes* which were worn over the fashionable padded hairstyles. The style of the crowns themselves was also affected by contemporary trends in architecture. The crown which Blanche of England, daughter of Henry IV, wore when she married the Elector Ludwig II in 1402 is, in its design, fully in accord with the elongated Perpendicular style of its near contemporary, St. Michael's Church in Coventry. The lower part of the crown is made up of medallions studded with jewels, and decorated, like the perpendicular windows, with delicate tracery. Above them rise the long and short pinnacles ending in a *fleur-de-lys* design, and again reminiscent of the pinnacles that punctuate the silhouettes of perpendicular churches.

By the mid fifteenth century a certain amount of jewellery seems to have been a social necessity for the respectable matron of good social position, and the low-necked dresses that had become fashionable made necklaces more important. Margaret Paston wrote to her husband in 1455 to ask for such a necklace, for when Margaret of Anjou was being received at Norwich: 'I durst not for shame go with my beads among so many fresh jaunty women'. Pendants, too, were becoming fashionable, and bangles suited the wide, loose sleeves of the fifteenth century. Devotional pendants followed the architectural styles closely, and goldsmiths produced outstanding work for the reliquary pendants. Rosaries, too, were frequently made of gold or carved coral. Crosses were often made up as part of a rosary, or worn as pendants, decorated with lobing or delicate *pointille* work.

We have already mentioned the supreme position of early Renaissance jewellery. The reasons for this supremacy are not hard to find. It is not merely a question of change of subject-matter, although this certainly took place. The subjects became classical rather than religious. The gothic pinnacles were replaced by classical columns. Instead of saints and figures from the Bible, we had Leda and the Swan or Hercules and the Nemean Lion. The real change was in the people who worked in jewellery. They had been talented craftsmen before; for a brief while they became artists. So many of the great artists of the early Renaissance had been trained in goldsmiths shops—Antonia, Pollaiuolo, Andrea del Cerocchio and Botticelli for example—that they had influenced the craftsmen who taught them with a desire to place jewellery on a higher level than had been the custom before, to make it great art on a small scale. The great name among artist/jewellers in England is Hans Holbein, who made designs for chains, pendants, silhouette enamels in moresque designs, hat jewels, etc. These were made, not by him, but by other Dutchmen in London and on the Continent.

One of the principal reasons why jewellery became so much more important was that the court in England, like those on the continent, was much richer than it had been. Henry VIII had taken over the vast riches of the Church in England for his own use, and Europe was beginning to discover the riches of the wider world. The most popular items of jewellery at the English court were pendants—especially heart jewel pendants—gold chains and collars. Hall, the chronicler, mentions the 'massye cheines and Curyous Collars' worn by the rich in his day.

The second phase of the Renaissance—mannerism—which elaborated and accentuated the features of the earlier phase, began to have an effect on jewellery in the 1560s. Simplicity and architectural values gave way to ornate display and even a certain vulgarity. The tendency towards profuse decoration was probably accentuated by the fact that jewels were now becoming the preserve of women rather than men. This was quite the reverse of established custom until the middle of the sixteenth century; Henry VIII had been far more magnificently bejewelled than his wives. Meanwhile, social gradations continued to be reflected in jewellery; the new styles might be seen at court among those who could afford to follow the whims of fashionable designs, but outside the court and its sphere of influence the earlier styles remained.

Unlike her father, Elizabeth used many English jewellers as well as foreigners. One of the finest was Nicholas Hilliard, who worked both as a designer and maker. His father, in the great tradition, had been a goldsmith and taught his son the craft. He probably designed the Heneage Jewel (V. and A.), which Queen Elizabeth gave to Sir Thomas Heneage in thanks for his services as Treasurer at War at the time of the Armada. On the front of the jewel is a bust of the Queen on a ground of translucent blue enamel. The rim of white enamel picked out in red and green stands away from the medallion and is set with rubies and diamonds. The back is enamelled with an emblem of the storm-tossed ark and a motto and, when it is lifted up, it reveals a miniature of Elizabeth by Hilliard. The inside of the lid is enamelled with a further motto and a rose within a wreath of rose leaves. The popular court jewellery of the late sixteenth-century included the carcanet and collar set, pendants, especially architectural pendants or those built up around baroque pearls, or ship jewels and portrait cameos more modest than the Heneage jewel.

Mannerism was succeeded by the Baroque and a new feeling for clear architectural lines. As the seventeenth century progressed, cut gems in profusion began to take precedence over enamelled gold, partly because of the introduction of the rose diamond cut in about 1640. Craftsmen continued to produce fine enamel work, but it was restricted to items such as watches and miniature cases.

Miniature cases were usually decorated in *champlevé* enamelling, a technique that had been popular during the Renaissance in which the metal base was hollowed out to hold the powder which formed the enamel. Watch cases might be treated in much the same way. At the beginning of the century they were often fretted or engraved; later they were shaped as shells, flowers or fruit, or they might be made of crystal and held together by delicate rims of gold. Pendants, on the other hand, were much more likely to be decorated with cabochon rubies or table-cut emeralds, or square-cut diamonds. Although it was the stones that were displayed when these pendants were worn, their backs were frequently finely enamelled, even if the gems used on the front were not very valuable.

Jewellery suffered an eclipse during the Commonwealth—naturally enough, for there were more important things to think about—but there seems to have been an increase in mourning jewellery. Jewels appeared in the form of *momento mori*, being either of general application, as were the coffin pendants, or commemorating particular people. The initials of a dead relation might be set on a ground of finely woven hair, or a picture of Charles I might be carried secretly.

The most characteristic jewellery of the eighteenth century was the parure: the matching set of earrings, brooch, necklace or clasp and ring, sometimes with a shoulder-brooch or buckle in addition. Its design reflected the change in the social habits of the jewellery-wearing classes. The time when a woman wanted to be seen at her most magnificent was at the evening gatherings in country houses, where the only light available was candlelight. Therefore her jewels must be designed to catch and disperse the light available, and this is what the diamond—and also the paste—parure did, thanks to the invention of brilliant cutting by a Venetian in about 1700.

The parure was by no means the only jewellery that was worn, however. Evelyn, in his *Mundus Muliebris*, lists many another fashionable trinkets:

Diamond buckles too,
For garters, and as rich for shoe . . .
A manteau girdle, ruby buckle,
And brilliant diamond rings for knuckle . . .
A sapphire bodkin for the hair,
Or sparkling facet diamonds there;
Then turquois, ruby, emrauld rings
For fingers, and such pretty things
As diamond pendants for the ears
Must needs be had, or 2 pearl pears,
Pearl necklace, large and oriental
And diamond, and of amber pale . . .'

Just as pastes and marcasites were used as alternatives to gem-stones, so imitations were made of gold, probably the best known being Pinchbeck, an alloy of copper and zinc. We can be grateful for this—quite apart from their own beauty—because most eighteenth century diamonds have been re-set and much of the previous metal used again in a new setting. Thanks to the fact that paste was not worth resetting, and Pinchbeck was left in its original design for the same reason, we still have examples of eighteenth century settings and of the pierced and chased Pinchbeck chatelains that would have been made in gold as well. Chatelaines were, of course, daytime jewellery. Their style changed continually from the one mentioned above, to the solid gold chatelaines of the second decade of the century, decorated with classical subjects in relief, to the painted enamel on gold of the 1770s.

Buckles were worn in the day too, and

Two tiaras of the Regency Period. Decorated with cameo heads.

were made variously of gold, paste, gilt metal and silver. The shoe-buckle became an important sign of a man's social standing, both at court and in the country church.

In the last third of the century, with the revival of classicism, there was a fashion for the paste copies of antique gems produced by James Tassie, and the cameos of Wedgwood mounted in rings or bracelets or set in gold chains.

The French Revolution and the Napoleonic Wars cut the English off from the influence of French design, and by the time contact was restored the English were set fair for the stale obscurantism demanded by the Victorians. There is no space to describe all the styles, only the mood, and the mood of early Victorian jewellery was backward-looking and sentimental. It was not the revival of ancient styles—Gothic, Renaissance, Algerian, Assyrian—that distinguished this jewellery, it was the lack of inspiration and creative thought with which they were revived. What the Victorians found attractive they adopted as their own and smothered in sentimentality. The Highland dress, which had been banned by the Hanoverians in the eighteenth century, was adopted as a fancy dress by the Victorians, and the business-like dirk became a bejewelled trinket. Mourning jewellery, in hair and jet,

took on a new and more macabre lease of life.

As the middle of the century passed, the revival of past styles continued, the jewellers paying more and more attention to accurate reproduction. Colour began to go out of fashion in the '70s, so that silver replaced gold, jet and ivory took pride of place, and diamonds, which had just been discovered in South Africa, supplanted coloured stones. Machines were largely replacing the craftsmen jewellers, and the age of expendable 'costume' jewels had arrived. Fashions became more flippant and more ephemeral. Childish novelties, like 'electric jewels' with moving parts, jewels in the form of beetles and ticks and grasshoppers, and sporting jewellery, were eagerly snapped up.

The reaction came at last, beginning with the amber beds of the aesthetes, gathering momentum with the Arts and Crafts Movement and the work of such designers as Walter Crane and C. R. Ashbee. The sinuous, lily-like lines of the Art Nouveau style began to affect jewellery, while stones cut *en cabochon* became the order of the day. The rejection of 'Victorian' fashions was far from universal, but it had a restraining effect even on popular jewellery, like the plain collars of ribbon or pearls that were fashionable in the later decades of the century.

181

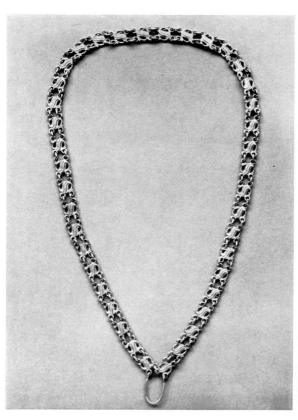

Left: *a rosary in gold with black enamel decoration. Dated about 1500. Above: a collar of SS silver. About sixteenth century.*

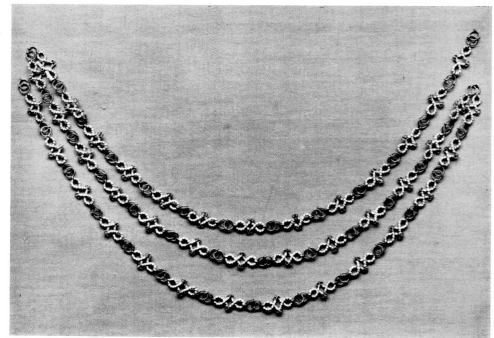

Enamelled gold chain, dated about 1600.

Armada jewel. Enamelled gold pendant set with diamonds and rubies. Dated about 1588.

Group of necklaces of gold set with amethysts, the lower set with pearls. These are dated 1830–1840.

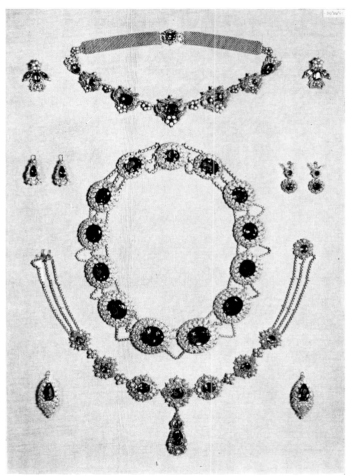

The brooch is cut and polished steel, mounted with an oval Wedgwood plaque of blue jasper dip with white cameo. Chatelaine, blue jasper and cut-steel beads with a plaque and pendants. Wedgwood. Dated about 1780–1800.

183

**Gold bracelet.
About 1840.**

Enamelled gold necklace and cross set with garnets and pearls. Designed by A. W. Pugin and dated 1848–50.

Gold tiara set with diamonds and pearls. First half of nineteenth century.

BOOK LIST

The following books are only a selection from a wide range of works on English antiques. They are recommended because they are not too specialised and have, in the main, been published within the past ten years so should be available. Almost all of these titles contain a bibliography.

A HISTORY OF ENGLISH CLOCKS
R. W. Symonds

AN INTRODUCTION TO OLD SILVER
Judith Banister

ARMS AND ARMOUR
H. L. Blackmore

ART OF THE GUNMAKER (2 vols.)
J. F. Hayward

BRITISH MILITARY SWORDS
J. Wilkinson Latham

BRITISH PEWTER
R. F. Michaelis

EARLY ENGLISH WATERCOLOURS
Iolo Williams

ENCYCLOPAEDIA OF BRITISH POTTERY AND PORCELAIN MARKS
G. A. Godden

ENGLISH CERAMICS
Stanley W. Fisher

ENGLISH CLOCKS
M. Goaman

ENGLISH COUNTRY POTTERY
R. G. Hagger

ENGLISH DELFTWARE
F. H. Garner

ENGLISH DOMESTIC SILVER
Charles Oman

ENGLISH GLASS
Sidney C. Crompton

ENGLISH GLASS
W. B. Honey

ENGLISH SILVER
Judith Banister

ENGLISH SPORTING GUNS
Macdonald Hastings

EUROPEAN CLOCKS
E. J. Tyler

FIREARMS
H. L. Blackmore

GLASS THROUGH THE AGES
E. Barrington Haynes

GUIDE TO MARKS OF ORIGIN ON BRITISH AND IRISH SILVER PLATE
Frederick Bradbury

BOOKLIST

GUN COLLECTING
G. Boothroyd

HOGARTH TO CRUIKSHANK
M. D. George

MILITARIA
Frederick Wilkinson

OLD ENGLISH PORCELAIN
W. B. Honey

PUBLICATION OF THE OLD WATER-
COLOUR SOCIETY'S CLUB

SMALL ARMS
Frederick Wilkinson

SWORDS AND DAGGERS
J. F. Hayward

SWORDS AND DAGGERS
Frederick Wilkinson

THE COLLECTOR'S DICTIONARY OF
CLOCKS
H. Alan Lloyd

THE COLLECTOR'S DICTIONARY OF
GLASS
E. M. Elville

THE ENCYCLOPAEDIA OF FURNITURE
J. Aronson

THE EVOLUTION OF CLOCKWORK
J. Drummond Robertson

THE ILLUMINATED BOOK
David Diringer

THE SMALL SWORD IN ENGLAND
J. D. Aylard

VICTORIANA
James Laver

VICTORIAN COMFORT
John Gloag

VICTORIAN FURNITURE
Simon Jervis

VICTORIAN VISTA
James Laver

WATER-COLOUR PAINTING IN BRITAIN
(3 vols.)
Martin Hardie

WEDGWOOD WARE
W. B. Honey

WEDGWOOD
Wolf Mankowitz

WORCESTER PORCELAIN
Stanley W. Fisher

INDEX